NOB
JOURN

"In *Noble Journey*, Craig Glass powerfully ....ons
every one of us are dying to talk about: se.. ....ı.., passion, pain, significance,
respect, doubt, and deception—just to name a few. On every page he reminds
us that what is truest and deepest about a man's heart is the noble image of
The One who invites us on a journey to become who we already are."
Michael John Cusick, Founder/President, Restoring the Soul;
best-selling author of *Surfing for God*

"Craig Glass has served for decades as a faithful guide for thousands of men and
their families. *Noble Journey* artfully offers up the accumulated wisdom of those
rich experiences, none more rewarding than how to live in freedom from shame."
Bruce McNicol, President, Trueface; best-selling co-author of *The Cure*

"I'm blown away by this book! Craig Glass completely reveals his heart in *Noble
Journey*, bringing insights and relevancy to the male wound, "Do I really matter?"
For anyone—man or woman—wondering if men are relevant, read this book.
For any men yearning for a renewed sense of passion in life, read this book!"
Jim Hinderliter, CEO, H2 Global Solutions

"In this book, Craig speaks to the core issues that cause men to feel disqualified. He offers hope that men can leave a life-giving legacy in spite of the
wounds we've received or the things we've done. As a father and husband, I
was encouraged and challenged by his words and hope you will be too."
Mark Aubin, Co-founder, Google Earth

"Over the past 20 years, I have known Craig Glass to be a man with a clear
ministry calling and impeccable integrity. This calling and integrity con-
verge in *Noble Journey*. There has never been a greater need for a voice that
challenges men to be the servant leaders God calls them to be. In this book,
Craig is that voice."
Kathy Maas, career ministry leader

"Craig has captured the essence of what a truly noble man is. This is the
man God created you to be—filled with passion, strength, and love. In *Noble
Journey*, Craig writes out of his years of digging into Scripture, pursuing his
own heart and the hearts of other men. His words are true, tried, and tested,
as is the noble man. I highly recommend this book."
Gary Barkalow, Founder, The Noble Heart;
author of *It's Your Call: What Are You Doing Here*

"Men face a wide range of stereotypes today but rarely are they biblical, godly, or even very accurate. Craig Glass has ministered to men for decades and understands how men matter, how significant their role is in the family, church, workplace, and society. His voice matters, and so does this book."
Stephen Macchia, President, Leadership Transformations;
author of *Broken and Whole*

"It has been my privilege to know Craig Glass for several decades. I can attest that the profound and creative wisdom he shares to help men know we really matter grows out of his own honest journey. This book is a whole-hearted invitation to become who we are meant to be. It's also a resource for the women in our lives so that together we can better understand our relationships. *Noble Journey* exudes life-giving wisdom!"
Wes Roberts, Master Mentor, Leadership Design Group

"In a day when the significance of the stereotypical, narcissistic, irresponsible 'man' is being questioned, this book has emerged to truly encourage this challenged gender. A man's man, Craig Glass knows the burdens men carry and the joy they can find in their identity as a passionate warrior class. He shows how they can not only be powerful, but also influential lovers of others; Kingdom-focused men of faith and courage who care about their families and leave a legacy of change for the better. I heartily recommend *Noble Journey*."
Tom Phillips, Vice President, Billy Graham Evangelistic Association

"This hardy book is a must-read for men who wish to impact the world in the most meaningful ways. But it isn't a book for men's eyes only. It is also a brilliant read for women who wish to see the men in their lives flourish."
Deb Gregory, spiritual director, curator of the *Betwixt Podcast*

"Craig Glass has taught me about manhood over some four decades, at times being my boss, confidant, advisor, counselor, and, most of all, friend. I know this book comes from a lifetime of reflection, gathered wisdom, and putting truth into practice. You will be glad you read *The Noble Journey*."
Brian Jose, Executive Director, Radstock Ministries

"I appreciate Craig's discerning mind and heart regarding the key issues of a man's journey with God. I am moved by the stories and the message of *Noble Journey*. Based on his life-long dedication to serving men, this is a compelling call to step into the fullness of who we are as men."
Bob Hudson, Founder/President, Men at the Cross

"Craig brings to life godly lessons full of transformational Truth, the kind that gives you courage to engage in the journey. I needed a boost and a boot; his words offered both."

Sam Froggatte, CEO, EyeLine Golf

"There is no shortage of books out there, but exemplars are hard to find. Craig Glass is one of those beacons of light helping to mold men all over the country. His words come straight from the heart, and he walks what he talks. He's the real deal!"

Alan Briggs, pastor, consultant, author of *Everyone's a Genius*

"Craig Glass's book will inspire men to rise up and pursue the high calling God has for them. He shares his own story of brokenness and vulnerability but also the thread of God's grace and goodness. *Noble Journey* will bring hope and courage to men to step up and into the noble journey of becoming the men their families and the world need them to be."

Jeanne Ley, LCSW; Director of Pastoral Care, Christ Church, Lake Forest

"In Craig's book we learn how significant men truly are. We influence lives—we affect others for better or worse. Craig's teachings have inspired me and I hope that men will use this book as a call to action to leave a legacy worthy of being called a Noble Journey."

Eddie Ainsworth, PGA; Executive Director/CEO, Colorado PGA

"In the many years I have known Craig, his single-minded passion has been to lead men on a noble and courageous journey of rediscovery and reclamation. This book is the culmination of that passion. One glance at the table of contents will clarify the battle and unveil the strategy to seize our God-gifted legacies."

Peter Burgo, Editor, *Alliance Life Magazine*, The Christian and Missionary Alliance

"In *Noble Journey*, Craig courageously and respectfully presents insightful truth that is rarely heard in a world that increasingly waters it down. If you're a man who longs to understand the depth of God's masculine calling—or a woman who cares about a man in your life—this powerful book is a life-giving roadmap for that journey. Buy it, read it, and live it!"

Vance Brown, Executive Chairman and Co-founder, Cherwell Software

"Craig Glass has spent his life exploring what it means to live out God's full vision for manhood. His thoughtful exposition on the topic is worth listening to as he is a humble warrior for the purposes of God in men's lives."

B. Joseph Leininger, Founding Partner, Resource Land Holdings

"With honesty and keen insight, Craig explores the truth that men matter and, when they walk in their God-given identity, they unleash their powerful influence for good. If you are a man who has ever asked the question, 'Am I significant?' *Noble Journey* answers with a resounding, YES!"

Leigh Davidson, freelance editor, David C. Cook

"As a result of the wisdom contained in these pages, my adult sons and I have developed a deeper bond as we've discovered the ancient ways of a noble man. This book is for every man who desires to be a better son, brother, husband, or father. I've known Craig for over 30 years as a friend, a leader, and a wise teacher. He's helped thousands of men reach higher and live more fulfilling and impactful lives."

Mark Dyer, leadership and ministry coach

"Craig is calling all men to fulfill our God-given purpose according to our God-given design. You'll find this read both inspiring and challenging."

Tom Yeakley, staff equipper, The Navigators

"No one cares for guys like Craig does. No one articulates guy issues in such a transparent way. Few men persist as he does with his passion to make men better and pass the baton well. Those who read this book will find their own struggles—and reasons for hope—in Craig's honest tales."

George Cook, Managing Director and Institutional Consultant, Graystone Consulting

"As a woman, I can only view men from my perspective, unless I stop long enough to really listen. We're just different from each other. That's why I recommend Craig's book to women (as well as to men). It's honest, well-presented, instructive. As I was reading it, I actually got out of my chair to find my husband and give him some overdue honoring encouragement. I would call this book a game-changer."

Debbie Johnson, blogger and author of *A Pocketful of Seeds*

"I've had the privilege of walking with Craig for several years. I've seen the impact of his ministry on the lives of men through his leadership, teaching, and authenticity. In *Noble Journey* he captures and presents these insights for a new generation of men walking this journey."

Tim Neff, Director of Procurement, Polaris Alpha

"Right now in America not many people are saying that men matter. Craig is a rare voice insisting that healthy men are vital to our society."

James Anderson, CEO, New Canaan Society

NOBLE JOURNEY

The Quest for a Lasting Legacy

CRAIG M. GLASS

Ownership of this book entitles you to free solo access to our
Noble Journey video teaching series, available at NobleJourney.org.
Please use access code: BEGINTHEJOURNEY.
Noble Journey is also a great tool for use in a group setting
to spark conversation and deepen friendships.
Register your group at NobleJourney.org/group

PEREGRINE

Acknowledgements

I'm grateful for the encouragement and investment of three people in particular in completing the vision of this book: my editor, Mike Hamel, for his guidance, insight and terrific talent with words; my proofreader, Leigh Davidson, for her sharp eye and great observations from a woman's perspective; and especially, my designer, life partner, and muse, Beryl Glass, for her unlimited support and artistic gift.

All Scripture quotations, unless otherwise indicated, are taken from the Holy Bible, New International Version®. NIV®. Copyright © 1973, 1978, 1984, 2011 by International Bible Society. Used by permission of Zondervan. All rights reserved.

Scripture quotations marked (NIV '84) are taken from the Holy Bible, New International Version®. NIV®. Copyright © 1973, 1978, 1984 by International Bible Society. Used by permission of Zondervan. All rights reserved.

Scripture quotations marked (NKJV) are taken from the New King James Version. Copyright © 1982 by Thomas Nelson, Inc. Used by permission. All rights reserved.

Scripture quotations marked (*The Message*) are taken from THE MESSAGE. Copyright © by Eugene H. Peterson 1993, 1994, 1995, 1996, 2000, 2001, 2002. Used by permission of NavPress Publishing Group.

Scripture quotations marked (RSV) are taken from the Revised Standard Version of the Bible, copyright © 1946, 1952, and 1971 National Council of the Churches of Christ in the United States of America. Used by permission. All rights reserved worldwide.

PEREGRINE

I dedicate this book to the men who have been brothers in my life, and to four mentors who demonstrated courageous leadership and unfailing kindness to others:

Neil Glass, my father and foremost male role model

Dr. Earle Fries, Bible scholar and pastor to missionaries

Dr. Walt Liefeld, church elder, inspiring teacher, and New Testament guide

Dr. Kevin Dyer, founder and president of global ministries serving the lost and suffering

CONTENTS

FOREWORD
By Stephen W. Smith

We live in a day when everyone claims they matter. Whatever our color, race, or gender, we are marching, picketing, shouting, and even fighting to say we matter. In all our efforts to prove this, we may not be considering how we lost our significance. How did we get so lost in a day and age when we have so much and have come so far?

To feel as if we matter is to have a sort of epiphany, a sort of awakening to the fact that we have dignity, worth, and value. In an age when technology, speed, and efficiency matter, our humanity is threatened. Machines are taking over. Robots are coming.

You are holding in your hands a message the world needs to hear! This book is a foundational and essential roadmap for men, and the women who love men. It is a guide to help us explore the heart, the core, the essence of a man, and the world that we have to navigate.

Craig explains the mystery of a man's heart—the inner world of a man—that sacred place where wounds lie buried; where the past so often enslaves a man for decades; where passion lies fallow and where making our lives count matters.

Noble Journey helps us look back, look up, look around, and look forward. Otherwise, we will live in a catatonic state of barely staying alive and live a life full of regrets. Too many men are living this way and Craig invites us to say, "Not me. I will live before I die. I will love deeply until the end. I will not live my one life alone. I will have a friend and be a friend. I will taste the goodness of life and of my God."

This book is born out of the wealth of wisdom and the years Craig has devoted to helping men know they matter. His track record includes both failure and success. Craig is transparent, showing his own failures, fears, and frustrations as a son, husband, father, and friend. He knows pain and through his pain you will be able to explore your own and find your way to wholeness again. He knows the issues that have tripped you up along the journey from boyhood to manhood.

The message within these pages is contagious. It will make you want to be a better man, a better son, a better father, a better husband, and a better friend—a man who is more alive than dead; a man who wants to thrive more than survive.

This is your invitation to sit with Craig and, as you read these pages, find a companion who, with the strength of a warrior and the tenderness of a caring friend, will guide you through the maze of your masculine heart to discover, explore, and own your dignity as a man.

Yes, dignity! There is dignity in being a man that is often buried by the shame that enslaves our hearts. Craig explains how to move from shame to freedom. Some men may want to flip to that chapter first because there is an epidemic of shame infecting the hearts of men including sexual shame, vocational shame, spiritual shame, and more. We need freedom and the road to it is clearly laid out here.

You will be taken back to your childhood and brought forward to face your legacy and death. You will ponder the vows you said to your wife and learn to close the gap that has somehow found its horrid way between you and her.

This is also a comprehensive guide for boys to become men; for those who have failed to be able to find their way back; for those who are stuck to get unstuck; and for those who are frozen and fearful of intimacy to experience true intimacy. For such a journey as this, we need this book.

I've been waiting for years for Craig to finish this manuscript! I've heard him give these talks. I've cried deeply as he led me and thousands of other men to look within and to look up for our help. I've witnessed his encounters with men and women dissecting the great themes of this book and I know the power of transformation we will experience by the encouragement Craig offers us through these pages.

This book should not be read alone. You won't want to read this by yourself. Get ten copies and ask your friends, your associates, and your team to read it with you. We need the insight, the reaction, the naked truth that Craig uncovers, and we need each other to find our way.

The male heart today is busted, shattered, and fearful of telling our stories to each other. We live alone, isolated, and we are dying inside for someone—anyone—to know us. This book is the invitation to tell our stories, our secrets, our fears, and our longings. This book is a tool to bring us together.

It takes a man to show us how to be men, and it takes a tribe of men to live this out and to reclaim what has been taken from inside us. We can do together what we cannot do alone. This book is the invitation to live this message out together.

Of all the men I have ever met, of all the voices that are speaking today telling us what to do and what not to do, of all the men who have the gravitas to tell us the truth, I invite you to know my friend, Craig Glass, and find your way home!

Author of *The Transformation of a Man's Heart, The Lazarus Life, Inside Job,* and *Soul Custody.* Steve lives in the mountains of Colorado and is the President of Potter's Inn, a Christian ministry devoted to the care of the souls of leaders in the marketplace and ministry. **www.pottersinn.com**

PART I
TRAILHEAD

CHAPTER 1

WHY MEN MATTER

Men don't matter.

As long as there are sperm donors available, kids can be raised just as well by a mom or two as by a dad and a mom. In fact, given the aggressive and noncommittal nature of men, it's probably best that they just stay out of the family picture.

In an August 2012 *New York Times* article, author Greg Hampikian made the point that "women are both necessary and sufficient for reproduction, and men are neither." He does acknowledge that his own father was the more influential parent in his life, but returns to his primary point of arguing the scientific irrelevance of men. "Ultimately," he asks, "the question is, does 'mankind' really need men?"

Men used to at least have a recognized value as the primary breadwinners and providers for their families, but that's no longer always the case. There are many households in our nation where women have become the primary providers. While that has been wonderful for unleashing the talent women bring to the workplace, it has sometimes had a secondary effect: another unspoken message that men have lost their significance.

When I'm not sure of my own impact as a man, I raise an eyebrow and wonder if these questions of male significance are accurate. When I'm reminded of the God-design of my heart and the potential I have for good in the lives of others, I want to disprove that message. When I'm listening well, I hear the longing for real men to "step up" that lies just beneath the surface of statements condemning men.

Do men really matter? That's not a question I learned to ask until more recently. But as I was growing up, I sometimes asked myself an even more personal, yet related, question: Do I have what it takes to be a man? And, by the way, what does a real man actually look like?

"AM I IN THIS PICTURE?"

When I was a freshman in college I was part of a great circle of buddies ranging from first-year students through seniors. We hung out together, played cards into the early morning hours, and told countless stories of our histories with women.

Several of us played on our dorm's intramural football team. I was chosen to be the quarterback and we hoped for a moderately successful season. Everyone knew that Third Floor East always won the championship, because they had the best QB, and they always hand-selected the best incoming freshmen.

As the season came to a close, our team and theirs went undefeated, meeting in the championship game. In true Hollywood fashion it went into overtime. As time was about to expire, facing fourth and 30 with the score still tied, I sent our receivers downfield breaking off to the right corner of the end zone. Except for one. Our running back and my best friend, Mike, delayed, crossed the line of scrimmage, and suddenly broke left. I pump-faked to the right, then drilled a pass to him as he streaked 30 yards under the whole defense for the winning score.

It was a sports achievement for the ages and a complete shocker. I was honored not only to be on the team, but also to be the winning QB. You would think that nothing could undermine my sense that I fit in with these men—that I mattered.

A few months later, as spring break approached, several of us sat in our dorm suite night after night and dreamed of a trip to Fort Lauderdale. There was one car available—an old VW Bug. There clearly wasn't going to be enough room for the six or seven of us who were regularly engaged in the nightly conversations. But, no matter, we all blissfully entered into the dream of sandy beaches, warm sun, and splashing surf.

Until one night when it became apparent the final list was being made and the five available seats were getting filled. Several of us continued the chatter and the storytelling while ignoring the obvious elephant in the room. Then, after all the other guys left, I asked my football teammate, Mike, who was tacitly in charge of the trip, "Mike, I just need to know: Am I in this picture?"

On the surface this might have looked like a question of logistics or physics. "Is it actually possible to fit five male bodies in a VW Bug?" But it was actually a question of significance.

Although it didn't come out this way, my question really was, "Mike, I realize that I was the QB, but I'm no longer sure that matters. I just need to know: Am I significant enough for you and the rest of the guys to get one of the most valuable seats in northern Illinois?"

Stunned at my question, Mike said with reassuring clarity, "What? Of course you're in the picture!" Relieved that at least for that trip I did matter, we went on to figuring out the physics question. (It turns out, five grown men can indeed survive a 3,000-mile trip in a Bug, as long as two are in the back, a sleeping bag is wedged between the two front bucket seats, the fifth man sits on the bag, spreading his arms on the shoulders of the guys to his left and right, straddling the gear shift, and the driver shifts with caution.)

When I asked Mike, "Am I in this picture?" I was really asking, "Do I matter to you?" That isn't the last time I asked another man that question.

And I'm not the only one. In my work as a minister to men, I regularly encounter men who question their value and competency. In fact, a deep hidden doubt in their ability to effectively manage their lives is one of the most common traits I see in men.

"I DON'T FEEL LIKE I MATTER."

Recently a friend who is a world-traveling businessman, and an honest struggler with his marriage and family, shared his frustration in an email:

Craig, I find the following:

- Lately I tend to be real quiet in family gatherings, in some ways like my father. After all, "even a fool who keeps his mouth shut is considered wise."
- My family does not seem to listen when I chime in on ongoing conversations.
- My older children seem to want to correct me on a variety of things, including listening in on me when I'm talking with house/dinner guests.
- It seems I receive more respect for my role at work than I do at home.
- I get lots of rejection when I try to pat my older sons on the back and speak positive blessing and encouraging words to them. They purposely sneer and jerk out of reach.
- It seems my older boys are angry with me. They enjoy my blessings of tuition help, buying meals and cars, etc. But I do not sense that they enjoy me as their father. They even question me about why I claim them as a dependent on my federal taxes.
- Perhaps my kids are responding in the same emasculating way my wife does in front of them or to our church pastoral staff.
- My boys always give my wife a hug and a goodbye when they leave, but tend to ignore me.

Succinctly, I really do not feel like I matter, I feel like a piece of shit...

Sadly, this state of affairs continues for my friend who, like many other men, lives with the pain of rejection and a sense of insignificance as a husband and father.

HOW DID WE GET HERE?

How can it be that we would literally be asking, and needing to defend, the question: "Do men have value?" Partly because we haven't been real men. We have fallen to our own worst stereotypes:

- *The Worker Bee Male* who makes career his first and foremost responsibility, downgrading his roles in his home, community, and church.
- *The Couch Potato Male* who goes inert at home and in the community, seeking refuge from the stress of a workplace that depletes his soul.
- *The WWF Male* who struts and poses his way through life, using intimidation, assault, harassment and anger to keep others in fear and under control.
- *The Cyber Male* who spends nearly as much time online as in the real world and who has deeper relationships with virtual people than with those with flesh on.
- *The Lost Male* who lives as though stranded on a remote island with no hope of rescue. He has no idea which stereotype is the authentic one. He dabbles in or rejects all of them.

Why do we default to these stereotypes? Every one of them is a different version of the same conviction: I'm not sure I really matter, so I'll compensate in ways that keep me safe or that impress others.

DOUBT AND DECEPTION

Despite the doubts some may have, the deep truth is men do matter. But it's just as true to acknowledge that many men don't think so.

I know this seems counter-intuitive. After all, we see so many examples of men who certainly don't seem to have any problem with self-esteem.

There are any number of sports stars who have all the acclaim, money and hardware the world can give them. There are plenty of ultra-wealthy businessmen managing their impressive portfolios and flying from one crucial board meeting to another. We rub shoulders with countless men who own the houses, drive the cars, and wear the clothes that culture tells us are the signs of success.

What do you mean men don't think they matter? Those guys sure do!

Early American philosopher and author Henry David Thoreau had it right when he stated over 200 years ago, "The great mass of men lead lives of quiet desperation." That's just as true today as it was in his time. The only difference is that today the desperation is just not as quiet.

How else can we explain the unbelievable risks so many men of power take to pursue that forbidden affair, to pad their wallets while others lose jobs, to bilk others of billions of dollars in pyramid schemes, to force their will or their bodies men or women under their authority?

If we look beneath the surface of many successful men we see clues that even they doubt their significance:

- How many Tour de France races does a champion need to fix through illegal blood doping until he's sure he matters? Apparently, more than seven.
- How many billions does a hedge fund manager need to swindle from people who trusted him with their life savings until he can rest in his significance? Enough to land him in prison for decades.
- How many buildings, helicopters, golf resorts, or airplanes with his name on them does a guy need to own before he can lighten up? We know at least one such brand name that is still counting.
- How many bedrooms, how many cars, how many suits, or how many affairs do we need until we can sit back, smile, and say, "That's enough"? Too many of us live in such a way that communicates, "At least one more."

Why are we doing this? Because there are two things in life men deeply long for:

Significance: To know we have impact, that our life matters, that because we lived the world is different. Our world teaches us that the main way of attaining significance is to accrue power (how much we control), to accrue possessions (how much we own), or to accrue prestige (what others think of us, or at least, what they think of our image). The route to all of these is performance.

Respect: To know that other men who know us not only like us, they respect us; they want to hang out with us. We want some kind of affirmation from other men that we are in the club, that we fit, we make the grade, we measure up as a man. Our world teaches us that the main way to do that is to promote what's impressive about ourselves, and, one more step, hide what's broken, fearful, or shameful.

Sadly, many Christian men fall for the same deceptions. Except that we also learn one more lesson: The last place to tell the truth about who we are, what we experience, what we fear, and where we fail, is church.

Why is that? Because while non-Christian men can revel with each other in their sexual appetites and conquests, or their self-gratification with alcohol, drugs, pornography, or other vices, we Christians feel compelled to demonstrate absolute victory over all of these.

We may not actually *have* victory; in fact, we may be as tempted and seduced by the world as the next guy. But we can't risk the shame, condemnation, or judgment that honesty might bring from our brothers.

As a result, we perform like crazy and we hide in fear. When our performance just doesn't seem to measure up, or worse, clearly results in failure, we think we no longer matter. When in isolation, we live in the shame of our own hypocrisy, lies, or self-condemnation; we are certain we no longer matter.

"I'M DISQUALIFIED"

In my work I regularly encounter men who question their value and competency. In fact, a deep, hidden doubt in their ability to effectively manage the requirements of their lives is one of the most common attributes I see in men.

A long time ago while doing men's ministry at a large church I met a 30-something man who seemingly had the world by the tail. He was the hotshot CEO of a growing company. He had a trophy wife, a beautiful home in the suburbs, and a red convertible Porsche that he drove at ridiculous speeds to work every morning. He apparently had it all together.

Until the morning I received a call from him saying with a trembling voice, "Craig, I'm on the shoulder of the expressway. I'm heading into a meeting with my board. They know everything. They know my lies, my cheating, and my cover-ups. I can't pull this thing off any more. They know the truth about me. I'm ruined." Then he burst into tears.

What's going on here? What's going on is that this man fell for the lie that his value is defined by success. Too many men believe that they matter to others solely because they have the external badges that prove their worth. At the same time they know the truth beneath the surface; they wrestle with fear, anger, confusion, and exhaustion.

Years later another man, Mark (not his real name), spent a weekend with me asking my help to determine a sense of calling and purpose for his life. Mark was well-educated, was raised in a solid Christian home and church environment, worked in a position of responsibility for a national financial firm, was happily married and the father of two children. He was the epitome of a successful man.

Yet as we spoke about his disengagement at church and why he was distancing himself from roles of spiritual leadership I sensed a familiar culprit: shame.

In revealing his story over time, Mark mentioned that he became a Christ-follower as a young boy and attended church regularly. In junior and senior high school he was a leader in his youth group. Adults viewed him as a wonderful example for his peers.

He regularly shared his faith with others and one day he invited a female high school friend over to his house for a Coke and to talk about what a life fully committed to Christ could look like. His parents weren't home, but Mark was focused on sharing his faith with his friend.

Predictably, their conversation strayed off course. They started talking more intimately and then began making out. Within a couple of hours they had had sex. Mark told me, "From that day on I've felt undeserving of ever serving in any spiritual leadership role. I'm disqualified."

That's shame talking. "You not only *did* something bad, your core defining identity is you *are* bad. You're more defective than anyone else. Cover up and compensate."

Christians who know they have erred spiritually hear this message of condemnation most piercingly. But men who might deny any faith at all also hear it. Each conscience hears its own negative soundtrack. Don't forget…

- What you did to those women in college
- What that man did to you as a child
- The abortion you insisted your girlfriend get
- That your dad said he was ashamed of you
- The middle school teacher who told you,
  "You'll never amount to anything good."
- The coach who demeaned you in front of every other guy who mattered to you

Men matter. We just don't think so. The voices of our culture, our teachers, our churches, and even our parents have far too often convinced us we don't count. In response we make choices that may seem understandable but are superficial and ultimately doomed to fail:

- We perform through production and perfectionism
- We impress through intimidation and violence
- We feign invulnerability through passivity and apathy
- We numb ourselves with pleasure and self-gratification

The internal conflicts men live with, the demands of keeping the secrets or keeping pace with expectations, result in men who either passively give up or violently take their rage out on others who least deserve it. You may know some men like this. You may be like this yourself.

If you're a man, I have good news for you, and I have sobering news for you.

The good news: You *do* matter. Despite the questions our society often raises about the value of men, and especially fathers (think Homer Simpson), you have a deeply important calling as a man. Your presence and your words have an enormous impact on those around you.

The sobering news: You matter. Your words and presence have impact, but that impact can go either way. It can bring life, security, and blessing into the lives of others, especially wives and children; or it can bring fear, shame, and violence.

MEN WHO MATTERED

When a man questions his own value, he completes the self-fulfilling stereotypes mentioned above. BUT when a man understands the charge he has been given by God, he enters into his calling. He changes internally and has deep impact externally.

Mr. Ledbetter was the first male teacher I ever had. He was the teacher all the seventh-grade boys hoped to get. The unlucky ones got Miss Hassman, an elderly, short-tempered woman who, when she suspected one of us boys as being the one who threw chalk sticks at the blackboard during lunch break, required all of us to go around a circle and respond, "It wasn't I." If we said, "It wasn't me," she kept us after school to wash blackboards anyway.

The fortunate ones got Mr. Ledbetter as their Home Room teacher. He spoke to us like men. When he addressed the boys alone in the room, as he did one morning, he said, "Gentlemen, I noticed a condom lying on the school grounds this morning. Do any of you know anything about that?" And then he would move into a lesson about life responsibility and self-discipline. "Gentlemen, I expect more from you." And you know what? He got it.

Mr. Schultz was my friend's dad. He was the president of his own company, an elder in the church, good looking, a cool dresser with a classy wife. I was on the swim team in high school. Most people at my church didn't notice. Mr. Schultz did. More often than not, on Sunday mornings during the swim season he'd come up to me and ask, "Craig, any races this week? How'd you do?"

This drew me to him like a moth to a light. I always knew where Mr. Schultz was.

If you took a minute, you could come up with your own stories about men whose words stood out to you. One way or another. They may have spoken shame, or they may have spoken significance. But I know you remember them.

Why is that? The words of a man are like the voice of God. Throughout Scripture God used men to anoint and bless others:
- Abraham blessed Isaac
- Isaac blessed Jacob
- Jacob blessed his son
- Eli blessed Hannah and Samuel
- Simeon blessed Jesus

Those who understand the hearts of men know that the only ones who can bestow blessing and anointing to men are other men. Women can provide exceptional gifts—comfort, companionship, inspiration, intimacy, and joy, but only men can bless other men. *It takes a man to convince a man he's a man.*

Here's the truth: In God's plan you have significance and meaning simply because you are a son of God. Let that sink in. You may like the way it sounds, but question it. You may doubt it outright. That's OK. It's still true. Men, you matter... and God has given you a calling that impacts the world.

Short of a miracle, another man's words will be the closest thing to God's blessing we will hear this side of heaven. Men, God has given us a high calling. We matter. Our presence, our words, and our actions touch lives and change the world.

We men know we *should* matter; we just doubt that we *do*. We pour enormous amounts of energy into the performance that results in the power, possessions, and prestige (or six-pack abs) that our culture tells us are the signs of significance. The betrayal is that, while we're convinced it works for everyone else, it clearly isn't working for us.

WHY MEN MATTER

Despite our doubts, I'm utterly convinced that we absolutely do matter. For four reasons:

1. *God's revelation of himself*

When God created humankind and revealed himself as a personal, loving God, he did so as a Father (Psalm 89:26; 103:12-14). He always used masculine pronouns in reference to himself. And when Jesus told the magnificent parable of the Prodigal Son, (Luke 15:11-32), he was revealing the heart of the Father. The image of God throughout Scripture is masculine.

That in itself places a spiritual mantle on men, fathers in particular, to be aware that we reflect God's revealed nature in every relationship we have. This is why the love, presence and touch of a man carries enormous weight—for condemnation or blessing.

Even non-Christian therapists know that most children's view of God is shaped by their fathers. A child with a kind, patient, present, loving Father can easily embrace those same qualities in God. She's familiar with them. The child with a distant, angry, vindictive, shaming father intuitively assigns those same qualities to God. He knows them all too well.

2. *Jesus's masculine presence*

When Jesus took on flesh and blood and confined himself to the limitations of humanity, he came as a male. He was a son and a boy who, "grew in wisdom and stature, and in favor with God and man" (Luke 2:52 NIV). He taught in the temple as young Jewish men did and surrounded himself with a group of men who became his brothers.

Jesus revealed himself as a man and in doing so gave all men a clear picture of who we can aspire to be. Kind yet filled with conviction. Connected deeply to the Father yet pursuing masculine community. Courageous enough to stand face-to-face with pious Pharisees (Matt. 3:7; 12:34), yet gentle enough to convince women they were entirely safe with him (John 4).

Jesus shows us how to be men. When we emulate him, we reflect godly, masculine qualities to others at home, at work, at church and in the community.

3. Fathers are the first "other"

Several Christian authors make the point that fathers are the first outside person a child has awareness of. A child is utterly connected with his or her mother through nine months of sharing the same body, through the life-giving umbilical cord, and through breast-feeding. In a baby's earliest development, he or she has no distinct awareness of a life separate from the mother.

The father isn't physically connected and he isn't the source of nurture in the intimate way the mother is, but he's there. He's the first "other" person who chooses whether to pay attention, connect, engage, talk to or hug a child. Whether he does or not makes an enormous difference.

A father's abandonment, absence or abuse can pass on a lifetime of woundedness. Conversely, his voice, love and presence can bestow a lifetime blessing (Genesis 49:25, 26). Fathers are the first influence that convinces a child whether she or he matters.

4. The impact of men on societies

"The most important question any society must answer is: How do we build good men?"

So spoke radio commentator Dennis Prager the day after the shootings at Sandy Hook Elementary School in Newtown, Connecticut. My first reaction was to question his opinion. Though I believe deeply in the value of men and their impact on society, I react instinctively against viewpoints that seem to elevate the innate value of one gender over another. I don't believe God does; neither should we.

And then I realized Prager is right. He is not talking about value; he's talking about consequences. In fact, my gut, my experience, and my own writing make the same case.

Women are so rarely the perpetrators of multiple crimes or violence. They far more often seem to direct their fiercest energy toward the defense, protection, provision, and security of those around them.

Fiercely violent and destructive men? The list is horrifically long. Compared to women, men have a disproportionately harmful effect on others.

Roughly half the world's population is male. We might assume then that roughly half the rapes, murders, thefts, and other acts of violence are perpetrated by men, and half by women. We hardly need to refer to evidence to know that assumption is absurd, but here it is: The United Nations Office on Drugs and Crime data show that worldwide, 85% of people convicted of assault are men, and 96% of murders are committed by men (www.unodc.org/documents). Men are by far the principal perpetrators of rape, war, torture, incest, sexual abuse, sexualized murder, and genocide.

Why do men matter? Because the difference between good men and wicked men is so extreme. Men seem to have a disproportionate outward impact on society, especially when it comes to violence. I believe it's just as true that men can have a disproportionate outward impact for protection, heroic self-sacrifice and blessing.

As a result, we men have a life-impacting choice to make: Will we direct our energy to bring blessing or destruction to those around us? Our answer affects the world.

That's a profoundly important message of truth, but it isn't the whole truth. The rest of it is that, as Soviet-era political dissident Aleksandr Solzhenitsyn points out: "If only there were evil people somewhere insidiously committing evil deeds, and it were necessary only to separate them from the rest of us and destroy them. But the line dividing good and evil cuts through the heart of every human being" (*The Gulag Archipelago 1918–1956*).

Every one of us has the capacity to make decisions that are self-serving or others-harming. The consequences of those decisions can be enormous.

At a Thanksgiving get-together in 2015 I told a group of friends of Peregrine Ministries, "We don't know when the next act of mass killing will take place, what weapons will be used or what location it will take place in, but we do know one thing in advance . . . the perpetrator will be male." We had no idea how soon this statement would be proven true in an incident very close to home.

The next day, November 27, a mentally disturbed man living on the fringes of society in Colorado killed three and wounded nine at a Planned Parenthood center in Colorado Springs where my wife and I live. That prompted a friend to ask me, "Why are the killers almost always men?"

When we pay close attention to the violent stories that surround us throughout the world, a pattern reveals itself. When wounded women lash out, they most often hurt themselves. They often direct their energy inward: suicide, prostitution, addiction, cutting, eating disorders.

On the other hand, when wounded men lash out, they most often harm others. They direct their energy outward: rape, murder, assault, slaughter, destruction.

There are exceptions to these broad descriptions, of course. There are some women who harm others outside their family, but those examples pale in comparison to the women who harm themselves, or even more horrifically their own children, perhaps the deepest act of self-hatred a woman can fulfill.

And certainly there are men who turn inward and commit suicide. At a very high success rate. But I think we can all agree that the pattern of mass killing, random destruction, sexual assault, domestic abuse and terrorism is an undeniably male-dominated phenomenon.

When people ask me how I came to the conviction that men matter, I tell them I came in through the "back door." The destructive impact of males in our society overwhelms the destructive impact of women. I believe that same powerful masculine impact can be turned toward good. That's the "front door."

Men matter precisely because the consequences of the character choices they make differ so significantly. Noble, other-centered men bring generational blessing to families and society; self-absorbed men bring multiplied destruction.

Our violent world desperately needs men who are convinced they matter for reasons far deeper than power, control, or destruction. When they do, they will be freed to use their strength, not for harm, but for the benefit of others. This is why we men have such a life-impacting choice to make: Will we direct our energy to bring blessing or destruction to others?

Our society questions the value of men primarily because it sees too many examples of broken men—men who pursue power, possessions or prestige. The world longs for men who have a clear sense of their own significance apart from the world's superficial measuring sticks. Men who use their strength, not for harm, but for the benefit of others.

Like it or not, men matter.

Let's make sure it's in the right way.

THERE IS HOPE, AND THIS BOOK IS FILLED WITH IT!

One morning I met with a young man and we happened to touch on the subject of pain and passion. I'm firmly convinced that there is often a direct link between pain we have experienced in life and passion we feel called to. When God heals past wounds, he does not erase the scar. He leaves a tender reminder that we were hurt in that place at one time.

Then he goes beyond healing when he redeems those scars and pain and turns them to passion. When embraced, admitted, and healed, our past wounds lead to compassion we feel toward others who experience the same pain.

I wanted to give my young friend an example. "You know how deeply I believe men matter. I write a blog by that title; I have a Facebook page called Men Matter. It's one of the deepest convictions of my life.

"Well, the truth about me is…" I paused. "The truth is…" I choked. Tears came to my eyes as I tried to regain my composure. It took a while. When I did, I finished the sentence, "The truth about me is, there are times I'm more deeply convinced that other men matter, than I'm convinced that I do. It's what compels me."

My pain: I'm not sure I matter.

My passion: I will do all I can to convince other men that they matter because I know what it feels like to doubt it.

The truth is that men have enormous value simply because we are men. Like women, we were formed in the very image of God. When he created us he breathed into us absolute, lasting, undeniable significance. He created us *on* purpose, *with* purpose. Men are no more valued or loved by God than women, but we *are* different. The world needs that difference.

The purpose of this book is to remind ourselves, in the face of a culture that constantly challenges us, that we matter far beyond the size of our bank accounts or the bullet points on our resume.

NOBLE JOURNEY

Men, if you long to establish a lasting legacy by focusing your attention toward others, you're on a noble journey. When I use the term noble in this book it's not as the noun that refers to a person's title of high standing in society. It's as the adjective that describes a person of integrity, deep character, and self-sacrifice.

A man of noble character has no need for selfish pursuits; he dedicates his strength and talents to the benefit of those around him.

If this describes your hope and intent, you're on the journey of your life. It's "a physical journey with a spiritual destination," in the words of author Daniel Taylor. This journey consists of long-anticipated milestones and shocking surprises, joy-filled summits and dark valleys, shattering losses and unexpected blessings. It is arduous and it is sacred.

Men matter. When we are humbly, yet clearly, convinced of the truth of that statement we can easily reject the false claims of significance that distract us and focus instead on the uniquely male calling God has in mind for us.

I invite you to join me on the journey.

Because you're in the picture.

And because you matter.

QUESTIONS
FOR FURTHER THOUGHT OR DISCUSSION

1. While men and women have equal value in God's eyes, and each gender wonderfully reflects God's nature, men carry a unique spiritual mantle on their shoulders. Do you agree with this theologically? Do you feel it personally? What does it feel like for you?

2. Dennis Prager says, "The most important question any society must answer is: How do we build good men?" What is your reaction to this statement? Do you think most men you know would agree with it? Would most women you know agree? Why or why not?

3. On pgs. 24-25 is a story of two men who made Craig feel like he mattered, simply because they paid attention. Has a man done this for you? What did he do to show belief in you? Who could you do this for you now?

4. How would you honestly evaluate your sense of either doubt   or confidence that you matter? Do you regularly struggle with doubts or shame about your innate significance? Or do you more often than not find yourself trusting in your God-given capacity to bring an impact of blessing to others?

FREEDOM FROM SHAME

When I was eight years old and my younger brother Clyde was three, we loved digging in the dirt in our back yard. We used several tools including a pitchfork with triangular-shaped tines and a shovel to dig holes, then jump in, and smear dirt onto our pants. It made us feel like men.

One fateful day in 1961 I decided to tease Clyde by pretending to stab him with the pitchfork as he sat in the hole. It seemed like a good idea at the time. Little did I realize that the next moments would mark both Clyde and me for many years to come.

I stepped back, grabbed the pitchfork, and raised it over my head. While making the most threatening growl an eight-year-old can make, I brought it down in Clyde's general direction.

What I *meant* to do was stick the pitchfork into the ground in front of the hole. I knew it would scare the daylights out of him and make for a good joke. What I *actually* did was bring it down just inside the hole—into my brother's knee!

Clyde shrieked in pain, blood spurted from his wound. I staggered back in disbelief at what I had done. I stared at his wound and dropped the pitchfork. After a moment of sheer terror, I shifted into self-protection mode. "Don't tell Mom!" I pleaded. What I thought he was going to do other than tell Mom I don't know.

Of course he ignored me and ran into the house screaming and bleeding. I counted on the fact that he was too young to explain what had happened. Knowing my mom would come running out of the house in moments, horrified, I concocted one of the most ridiculous series of lies in the history of sibling rivalry.

Sure enough, my mother came racing around the corner of the house, panicking.

Mom: Craig, what on earth happened to Clyde's knee?!

Me: We were playing in the dirt and he jumped into the hole and…I think something sharp stuck him in the knee.

Mom: Something sharp? What was it?

Me: Uh…it was a bunch of wires in a cable.

Mom: How could a cable of wires make a triangular hole?

Me: (Feverishly, I invented the next lie almost as quickly as my bewildered mother posed the next question.) I guess they were sticking out in the shape of a triangle. (Did I mention this was the most ridiculous series of lies in history? It gets worse.)

Mom: Let me see it. Where is it?

Me: Oh…I, uh…I took it out and reburied it.

Mom: Buried it! Where?

Me: Underneath the bushes back by the alley.

How I could have dug the cable out and reburied it 50 feet away, then run back to the scene of the crime in the 30 seconds it took Mom to come out of the house escaped me. I don't think it escaped her. I can only assume that by then my Mom's patience and belief in me was gone because she only said, "You can show Dad when he gets home."

When Dad got home 45 minutes later, he explained that the doctors needed to know what exactly made the puncture in order to treat Clyde's wound. Having no idea how I was going to lie my way out of this, I led Dad across the back yard to show him the imaginary hole where the imaginary cable of triangular shaped wires was fictitiously buried.

I was in the midst of coming up with the lie I would tell when we found the imaginary hole was empty, when suddenly there was a crack of thunder and light rain started to fall. I couldn't believe it! God was on my side! He answered my unspoken prayer request and rescued me!

My dad and I halted in the middle of the yard and he simply said, "OK. We'll have to take a look later when it stops raining." That was the last conversation we had that day. My parents never brought up the subject again the rest of my life. Nor did Clyde.

Yes, my series of lies saved my skin, but what I didn't know then, which I learned much later in life, was that on that day I put on a cloak of shame. I learned there was something deeply deceitful in me. I learned to become a liar and to cover up who I really was on the inside.

For years—decades in fact—every time I saw my brother in basketball shorts (and he played basketball through college and beyond), tennis shorts, or a swimsuit I saw that triangular scar on his knee, and I was reminded of the darkness of my soul.

Let me say it again. On that day in 1961 I took on a cloak of shame, custom-made for me, and it fit very well. I took on the hidden belief that there is something uniquely broken, dysfunctional, and dark about who I really am that isn't true of other people. Just me. My identity is unacceptable and it must be hidden.

I was a Christian; my sins were forgiven because Jesus died for me. I knew that, but it almost didn't matter because this was about something else. This was not about the destination of my soul; that was taken care of. This was about the quality of my soul, the quality of my identity, as a boy and then as a man. It was dark and it must be covered up, lied about, and compensated for.

This is what I mean when I talk about shame.

WHAT SHAME ISN'T

When I refer to shame in this chapter I want to clarify what I'm not talking about:

Shame is not lack of decency. The way I'm using the word shame is not the way it is commonly used to describe public decency or a sense of decorum. This use of the word shame is actually appropriate to describe an emotion. We hear people say things like, "Young people today are shameless," or "Businessmen who use shady practices have no shame."

That's not how I'm using the word. The shame I'll describe is so dark and wounding that I don't even like using it in any other way. I'd rather call this lack of decency just that: Lack of morals or decency.

Shame is not the same as guilt. Guilt is about behavior; it's black and white. You're either guilty of a certain action or you're innocent. It's a behavior or action that is undeniably true. In my case I stabbed my brother. There is no denying it, try as I might. It was simply true of me. I was guilty.

The Holy Spirit convicts us of our guilt and God forgives us. Because the price has been paid, the penalty for our sin is removed as far as the east is from the west (Psalm 103:12).

Shame is not based on external behavior; it's an attack on internal identity. Shame is not clearly black or white, it is shrouded in a gray haze that we are virtually blind to. It is full, not of conviction, but of condemnation. Far from being the truth, it is a lie about us. And the primary voice is not from the Holy Spirit. The primary voice of shame is from Satan himself, the author of lies.

I was guilty of stabbing my brother with a pitchfork. I knew God forgave me, but the shame of what I did, the shame of the tapestry of lies I wove, designed a custom-fit cloak that I wore and even added to for many years afterward.

Some of you might be asking yourself, "Do I have shame about my identity?" Perhaps you haven't seen anything like this in your life yet. You're blessed. I think some people are graciously protected from shame. My wife Beryl is. She is the least shame-based person I know. When I first met her, I found her freedom from shame to be one of her most attractive qualities. That appreciation has only grown over the years.

Others of us are not as fortunate. When we read this description of shame and what it feels like, we are very familiar with it. My experience in ministry the past 41 years is that almost all of us carry some of this self-condemnation as if it were a weight in our own backpack. Some of us may hardly be aware of it, but others can tell we carry a weight. Others of us are all too aware of the reoccurring messages of self-condemnation we hear, and the corresponding messages of self-motivation we keep repeating.

My experience is that most of us are in one of these two groups.

WHAT SHAME IS

What is shame and where does it come from?

Shame is the belief that we don't measure up. One of the best books dealing with shame is Lewis Smedes' *Shame and Grace.* I highly recommend it. It is one of the resources God used to help me get a better understanding of the impact of shame in my life. Many of the following observations I first learned from Smedes.

Smedes says: "Shame is a very heavy feeling that we don't measure up...The feeling of shame is about our very selves not about something bad we said or did but about who we are. It tells us that we are unworthy. Totally."

Shame is the belief that if others know the truth about me, they will abandon and reject me. At its heart that message is a lie. But we believe it's the truth.

We hear it in these words of John Quincy Adams, one of the greatest statesmen in American history who wrote, "My life has been spent in vain and idle aspirations, and in ceaseless rejected prayers that something beneficial should be the result of my existence."

That's shame talking. This from a man who served his country as ambassador to Holland, Great Britain, and Russia, as well as secretary of state, senator, and president.

We even see its presence when we read a bumper sticker that says, "Lord, please help me be the person my dog thinks I am."

My story of shame began when I was eight and it involved a pitchfork and a brother. Yours doesn't, but is there a story like this you could tell? For some of you it's repeated many times over in various forms. For others it's subtler. For still others it's a story filled with darkness and self-judgment.

Before going further I want to say, if you have never made the decision to accept God's forgiveness for your sins, I imagine the weight can be more than you can bear at times. I urge you to come to terms with God's forgiveness for you. The price has been paid through the death of the only perfect person who ever lived. His name is Jesus.

For those of us who are Christ-followers, when we're honest we admit that we still have doubts, fears, and deep disappointment about the quality of Christians we are. We know we're forgiven, but we struggle to believe we are fully accepted. We know God loves us, but we are also convinced that deep down he is terribly disappointed in us. That is shame talking.

Shame is the source and the consequence of sin. Shame is the heavy mask that covers our doubt as to our identity in Christ. If we scratch beneath the surface of just about any self-protective or sinful behavior common to men, we'll find shame. We hide our shame behind numerous masks:

- We become perfectionists; deep inside we have flaws we want to cover up.
- We become workaholics, compensating for a lack of worth by pursuing success.
- We intimidate others with anger and violence lest they see our fear or weakness.
- We retreat into passivity, taking no chances that we might fail once again.
- We pursue addictive behavior to comfort and quiet the voices of condemnation.

All of these masks are broken attempts to satisfy God-given longings. The perfectionsist is longing for acceptance. The workaholic is longing for admiration. The intimidator is longing for respect. The "passivist" is longing for safety. The addict is longing for peace.

We doubt our deep intrinsic value and we believe the lie that there is something uniquely broken, dysfunctional, and irreparable about us. We choose a sinful response that keeps us safe, compensates for failure, or comforts, but only temporarily.

And shortly after, we encounter the familiar attack against our character and identity, only it's fresher and deeper this time. In doing so, we stuff another rock of shame into the backpack. We put yet another layer on our cloak of shame.

You think you're the only one and no one must know, least of all, any other Christians. You have learned that church is the last place you can tell the truth. You sit here on Sunday, but you know where you went on the Internet two nights ago. If anyone else knew, they would turn on you. That's shame.

You allowed the rush of getting ready for church to cause you to lose your temper and lash out at your wife and children. The weight of self-condemnation feels terribly heavy. That's shame.

You took sexual advantage of a girl, or a boy, as a young man, then abandoned them. No one must ever find out what you did. That's shame.

You are that boy, victimized by someone you trusted. Now you sit here with self-condemnation that won't go away. That's shame.

Let me be clear, I'm not letting us off the hook here. Most of these examples involve sin that deserves conviction and requires repentance. But for Christ-followers, these sins don't deserve condemnation. And there are few places more condemning than some churches.

While we may know we're forgiven, we have deep doubts about whether we are acceptable yet. No one, least of all fellow Christians, must ever find out the truth about us. We learn to keep sin hidden, make up for it, compensate, dull the pain. That's shame.

We choose to rely on selfish or harmful behavior to dull the pain of shame rather than to accept who God sees us to be. We sin. There is short-term relief but long-term shame. Soon I want to dull the pain again. And on the cycle goes.

Shame is both the source and the consequence of sin. And the Enemy loves it; he laughs and celebrates this dark cycle.

WHERE SHAME COMES FROM

In the grand scheme of things shame entered the biblical picture very early on when Adam and Eve betrayed God's trust by eating the forbidden fruit in the Garden of Eden. (Christians disagree as to whether this story recounts a literal, historical event or is a metaphor that describes the sinful state of humankind. For the purposes of this book, we won't delve into that argument, but regardless of one's interpretation there are spiritual lessons we can apply today).

The story in Genesis 3 tells us that Adam and Eve immediately noticed they were naked and they covered themselves up. It's like they realized, "I am now exposed for others to see. There is something about me that must be hidden, even from God's eyes."

When God called to Adam and Eve they hid themselves because they were ashamed. And when he confronted them with the question of what they had done, they responded with shame-soaked excuses.

Adam says, "The woman you put here with me, she gave me some fruit…" What he means is, "It's her. She's to blame, and truth be told, God, even you are partly at fault for giving her to me."

Eve is no better: "The serpent deceived me."

Adam blames Eve. Eve blames the devil.

Shift the blame. Hide. Cover up.

And with that encounter, shame came to the human race.

This is the root of shame, but there are more familiar sources.

Secular culture. All you have to do is watch TV to see a series of messages that are, at their heart, shame-filled. Even the commercials repeat a familiar message: What you have, what you own, where you live, what you drive, how you look, how you dress, how you smell, simply does not measure up. There is something wrong with virtually everything about you.

You fall short of our culture's minimum standards. Shame on you!

Graceless religion. In their encouragement of a Christ-like lifestyle many churches pass on a message that is more about performance than about grace.

Smedes says, "A person can catch a healthy case of shame in church." I sure did. I grew up in a very conservative church background where only men were allowed to speak or teach; women were silent and wore head-coverings. There was no pastor.

One day when I was about ten, still learning to live with the shame of that pitchfork thing, I was cornered by a scary old elder of the church who confronted me with the following encouragement: "Young man, every man in the church must be ready to preach, pray, or die with ten minutes' notice. Are you?"

I never said a word in response, but in my heart I thought: Preach, pray, or die? Are you kidding? Those are my life options? Let's see, well if you knew anything about me and pitchforks, even *you'd* agree it wouldn't be preaching. I don't speak King James English so it isn't pray. I'll guess I'll take door number three: death.

The story has a sadly humorous tone now, but I can assure you, that day I added a cloak of spiritual shame to my wardrobe. My conclusion: I must not be a real man.

Unaccepting parents. One of my best friends in junior and senior high was Tim, a fellow member of the swim team. One thing about swim practices is that they are mind numbing to watch. Even those of us in the pool who are throwing one arm after another ahead of our body need frequent changes in the routine. Four or five thousand yards of swimming gets old fast—especially for those watching.

My father, who worked in Chicago about 60 minutes from my high school, came to almost every swim meet during my childhood and high school "career." There were numerous times when I would grab my breath underneath my arm stroke at practice and catch a watery glimpse of my father sitting in the stands. It became such a common sight it was no longer shocking. It's one of the ways I learned as a boy that he loved me and was proud of me. It's one way I learned that I mattered to him.

In four years of high school I never saw Tim's dad at a swim practice. Apparently what his son was doing in the water for hours after a long day of classes didn't matter to him. Understandable enough. But, not only did he never show up at practice, in four years of about 20 swim meets a year, I never, ever, saw his dad at a meet. Unforgivable.

Tim never complained; he never got angry that I could tell. But the contrast between the attention so many of us got from our cheering parents and the stark absence of his father had to go deep. I'm afraid Tim caught a case of shame during those years.

The Enemy. The seed of our shame began in the Garden; that seed is planted and watered by our secular culture, by graceless churches, and by unaccepting parents. But the true nurturer of our shame is the Enemy himself.

Satan takes that seed and covers it in the dark soil of hiddenness, fertilizes it with self-condemnation until it grows into a weed that wraps around us and clings to our view of ourselves.

THE REST OF THE PITCHFORK STORY
When I was 43, 35 years after I introduced my brother to the business end of a pitchfork, I realized for the first time this was a story that had brought me self-condemnation because it had always remained hidden. It was time to shed light on it; get it out of the backpack. I decided to call my brother, and then my parents, to confess and apologize for one of the darkest incidents of my childhood. (But not THE darkest).

I called Clyde, who lives in Canada, by then a man of 38 himself.

Clyde, I need to confess and apologize for something I did to you. I betrayed you many years ago and I've been reminded of it countless times. Over the years it has become a secret I could never speak about, but I need to get it in the open.

Remember when we were boys digging in the backyard; you hurt your knee and you have scar there to this day? I want to make sure you know that I did that. I stabbed you with a pitchfork. It wasn't on purpose, but I lied through my teeth to keep anyone from ever finding out. I'm so sorry, Clyde. I never apologized, and I just need you to know it was me who did that to you.

His response, with a chuckle: "Yeah, I know. Pretty crazy, wasn't it? That's OK. It's no big deal."

I sat in stunned silence. For 35 years, it was…no…big…deal.
I moved on to my parents, then living in Florida, for whom this ad-

mission of my guilt and shame would take significant courage. No telling what their reaction might be after three-and-a-half decades. I knew they would be gracious, but I feared for how hard this might hit them. After the initial pleasantries I finally brought it up:

> Mom and Dad, do you remember when Clyde and I were boys he got his knee punctured and it left a scar?
>
> Confused, they said, "What?"
>
> The scar. The triangular scar on Clyde's knee. Remember when that happened?
>
> Silence, and then, "No. What are you talking about?"
>
> What?! You don't remember?

I then launched into an incredulous recounting of the story that stands out to me more than just about any story of my childhood. I admitted my actions, my lies, my guilt, and my shame.

"We're sorry, honey. We don't remember anything like that."

They had no memory of it! For them it was forgotten as if it had never happened.

Friends, this is what God does with our sin.

The Enemy relishes capitalizing on our guilt, convincing us that though it may be forgiven we are still unacceptable because our guilt is darker than anyone else's. If the truth is uncovered, we will be rejected and abandoned by those who mean the most to us. Especially by God.

And it's a lie! The conviction of my sin was justified, but the condemnation of my sin was a lie. And, men, so is yours.

The truth is, it's *forgotten* by a forgiving God! Not only the guilt is forgiven, not only the shame, but the whole incident itself. Hebrews 10:17 says, "Their sins and unlawful acts I will remember no more." He has no memory of it!

HEALING OUR SHAME

How do we move from the cycle of shame to genuine healing? There are several steps.

We embrace grace. The beginning of healing from shame is under-standing that, as Smedes writes, "We are accepted by the Grace of the One whose acceptance of us matters most." We remind ourselves that God's unconditional love brings not only forgiveness, it brings complete acceptance. His view of us is not tainted by condemnation; it is defined by grace.

Friends, we are not only forgiven, we are accepted by the One whose acceptance lasts for eternity. Never to be rejected or abandoned. That's it; that's all; that's enough.

Or it should be enough, but shame returns.

Because the shame-based lies of our culture are so frequent, the messages from parents go so deep, the performance of religion is so convincing, and the whispers of the Enemy are so insidious, shame often returns.

Sadly, sometimes embracing grace isn't enough.

We believe what God says about forgiveness and acceptance. We need to soak ourselves with the truth of God's words about us. I've already referred above to Hebrews 10:17 but I want to point out that the whole chapter is fully given to reminding Christians that while the animal sacrifices of old were repeated annually, the sacrifice of Jesus is once for all.

Psalm 103:12 reminds us that, "as far as the east is from the west, so far has he removed our transgressions from us." When God views us he does not see men wrapped in sin, he sees the blood of his Son. Jesus' sacrifice is so powerful and eternal that our sin is eternally removed from us.

We accept what God says about shame. Romans 8:1 reminds us, "Therefore, there is now no condemnation for those who are in Christ Jesus." Or as *The Message* puts it, we "no longer have to live under a continuous, low-lying black cloud."

No condemnation! Conviction? Sure. That's comes from the Holy Spirit. His conviction is about our behavior, actions we have taken that are clearly sinful. That gets forgiven and forgotten.

Condemnation? None. Condemnation attacks our value and worth in God's eyes. It is not about behavior; it's about identity. It comes from the Enemy, and it's a lie from the pit of hell.

Psalm 25:3 affirms that, "No one who hopes in you will ever be put to shame…" Look at those words, "No one," "ever." They are pretty inclusive. None of us who place our hope in the name of Jesus will be put to shame. Ever.

Then there's Psalm 34:4–5: "I sought the LORD and he answered me; he delivered me from all my fears. Those who look to him are radiant; their faces are never covered with shame."

Shame in our lives causes enormous fear, secrecy, and insecurity. When we pursue God, he frees us from all of these. When we look to him and fully receive the unconditional love he extends, it brings a smile to our lips. It brings a sparkle to our eyes. It brings joy. Our faces turn radiant.

Those of us who are his children need never have faces covered in shame. We may forget God's forgiveness, or we may stumble over Satan's lies about us. But if we remember who we are, how God feels about us, and what his Word says about us, our faces are never covered in shame. How often? Never!

But sadly, sometimes reminding ourselves of the truth in God's Word isn't enough. Shame returns. Then what?

We invite trusted friends into our journey. We cannot experience freedom from shame in solitude. Shame grows in darkness, secrecy and isolation. It dies in the light, grace and support of being known and loved by a community of men.

I John 1:7 says, "But if we walk in the light, as he is in the light, we have fellowship with one another, and the blood of Christ, his Son, purifies us from all sin."

Men, when we walk openly, in the light of God's guidance, and the light of authenticity about our lives, two marvelous consequences take place. We experience fellowship with those we entrust with our struggles; and through the blood of Christ we experience transformation.

Many men, perhaps most, suspect the exact opposite will happen if they tell the truth: they will be condemned and shamed even more. Sadly, many men have found that to be true in their churches or with their Christian friends.

That should *never* be the reaction of mature, honest men to any-one's story. The reaction, as this verse clarifies, should be deeper community and deeper spiritual growth.

This verse is an encouragement to those of us who dare to tell the truth. And it's an exhortation to those of us with whom a friend trusts his truth.

We renounce shame. Repeatedly. Verbally. Pray often against Satan's efforts; out loud so he is certain to hear it.

There is no reason the enemy shouldn't continue his attacks on us. It makes the most sense from his dark perspective that he would. Why not? He won't hesitate. In the same way, there is no reason for us to hesitate to pray against those attacks. That shame has become like a cloak around us. It has taken years to collect it. It may take years to finally be freed of it.

It has become so conformed to us that sometimes we think it IS us. It's not. We must pray that God removes it, separates us from it. Takes it away and burns it in the trash heap where it belongs.

In the movie, *The Mission*, Robert De Niro portrays a Spanish conquistador in Latin America. He is guilty of rape, murder, and the slaughter of innocent natives in his quest for adventure. After some life-altering experiences through which he begins to see another perspective of his awful behavior, he remorsefully joins a Catholic order.

But his shame remains with him. He takes his battle armor, helmet, sword, and knives and stuffs them into a huge sack he ties onto his back in self-imposed penance for sins he was convinced were unforgivable. For days he carries the weight of this heavy reminder on a pilgrimage with his spiritual brothers along jungle trails, through rain-filled muddy creeks, and then climbing a sheer rock cliff to the top of a summit.

Finally at the top, nearly dead from exhaustion from carrying his shame, he encounters not just his brothers, but the tribe of natives he has committed some of his worst crimes against. Covered with mud and sweat he crumples defenseless at their feet. One of the tribesmen pulls a knife and holds it to his throat. De Niro's conquistador accepts his fate. It's over. He deserves what's coming. His sin and shame are too great.

The native pulls back De Niro's head exposing his throat and quickly swipes the blade through the hemp rope, releasing the sack of shame, which falls to the ground. Overcome with grace and the emotion of the moment, De Niro shudders with great sobs, which slowly, but surely, turn to laughs of joy as those who had every right to condemn him to death embrace him instead.

It's a remarkably powerful illustration of the release of self-imposed shame, and I encourage you to watch it.

Men, when we are freed from the shame of self-condemnation, we feel release, freedom, and joy. Our response to God's amazing grace should be to embrace the truth about who we are. We are his sons. We should welcome his eternal forgiveness and acceptance.

Renounce shame. Embrace grace. Remind yourself of the truth of God's Word. Invite trusted friends into your journey. Remove that greasy, hairy cloak of shame. Empty the backpack filled with reminders of your sin.

And for goodness sake, get rid of that pitchfork!

QUESTIONS
FOR FURTHER THOUGHT OR DISCUSSION

1. How did this chapter help you understand the key differences between guilt and shame? What are they?

2. Shame can be produced by: Secular culture, graceless religion, unaccepting parents, the Enemy. Can you identify the source of any shame you have carried with you in life? What's the source? What message does it whisper to you?

3. We hide behind masks that seem to work for us in covering shame. Do you know what masks you use to cover up or compensate for shame?

4. Healing from shame first requires acknowledgement that we are wounded, often an extremely difficult step for men. Have you ever thought you have wounds? Do you acknowledge them or prefer to move on? Or are you tired of acknowledging them?

5. The steps to healing are: 1. Embrace grace. 2. Believe what God says about forgiveness. 3. Believe what God says about shame. 4. Bring friends into your journey. 5. Renounce shame, verbally, repeatedly. Where are you in these steps? Which is especially hard to do?

6. Granting forgiveness is primarily for your benefit, but it requires knowing whom to forgive. Have you been, or are you, able to forgive the one(s) who have harmed you? If not, can you identify what's stopping you?

CHAPTER 3

LIVING IN PURITY

Remember the book *Men Are from Mars; Women Are from Venus*? It became a best seller and opened up an honest conversation of the innate differences in the ways men and women think, feel, and behave. In a society that often tries to promote the belief that there *are* no differences, other than those that have been culturally forced upon each gender, it was an encouraging secular example of admitting the truth.

It is true men are from Mars, the planet named after the Roman god of war. On a cellular level we tend, more than most women, toward competition, strength, impact, destruction, and initiating action.

It is true women are from Venus, named after the goddess of love and beauty. There is something on a cellular level that gives most women greater abilities than most men in the areas of feelings, communication, relationships, love, accepting, and attracting others.

These God-designed gender distinctions are nowhere more evident than in how we approach and live out our sexuality, and in what draws us into temptation.

THAT WAS THEN; THIS IS NOW

Several years ago I traveled internationally on a regular basis. It was not uncommon for me to be gone two, three, even four weeks on my own visiting missionary teams in different parts of the world. One time I had the unusual pleasure of being accompanied by my wife, Beryl, and my 13-year-old daughter Barclay for part of a trip.

For ten days we visited the UK, Germany, then Austria, where Barclay had been born. We had a wonderful time, but when they headed home my heart ached with the desire to go with them, or for them to continue with me. My next destination was Moscow, a dreary, gloomy, depressing place back in those days just after the fall of the Iron Curtain.

On top of that, my job there was to help mediate and resolve conflicts that had developed between team members. After the joy of time with my family it wasn't exactly where I wanted to go next. I finished my work and a few days later found myself in one of the older and more run-down parts of the Moscow airports that served only destinations in the far-flung Central Asian Soviet Republics. I was headed to Almaty, Kazakhstan at the base of the Himalayas.

As I stood in the check-in line at midnight, surrounded by only swarthy, bearded men, and women in flowing robes and head coverings, I felt entirely out of place. After resolving a complicated process at the counter I noticed the one other western-looking person in the whole airport also struggling with the same process at the counter next to me.

She was a young French woman, traveling alone, who spoke only French and English. I was able to help resolve the misunderstanding before leaving for my gate.

She arrived at the same gate a few minutes later and sat next to me. When we boarded our flight I sat next to a window. There were no assigned seats and, again, she chose to sit next to me. I didn't really mind. Did I mention she was French? And that she was quite attractive?

What followed was one of the most surreal and unexplainable experiences of my life. The flight was delayed. While we waited, she and I talked; we got to know each other's background; we told each other about our families; we became traveling companions.

The flight finally took off around two in the morning. It was pitch black, but as we pierced through a heavy cloud cover, we entered into another world—sparkling stars, a bright full moon, a thick blanket of illuminated clouds beneath us.

Never before or since have I had such a sensation of leaving one reality beneath that barrier of clouds, and entering a completely different reality. What was down there in the misery that was Moscow and Kazakhstan was one life; up here was a separate one.

Did I mention I was sitting next to an attractive, engaging, French woman traveling alone? We talked, we laughed, and as people do when they travel through the night, we slept next to each other. My mind entertained a variety of fantasies that I knew would never happen. And they didn't. I was on a mission trip, for Pete's sake.

We landed in Almaty, walked across the tarmac toward baggage claim together and said goodbye. She was greeted by a male friend; and I, by the team leader waiting for me to resolve yet another missionary conflict. That was nearly 20 years ago and of course we never saw each other again. But she made an impression on me.

Now, I ask you, what in the world was that all about?

I was a committed Christian. I was happily married with a wonderful family. I had just enjoyed a once-in-a-lifetime trip with my wife and daughter. Yet, I found myself unwittingly vulnerable to a temptation that, if acted on, would have compromised everything.

Never have I felt more strongly a sensation that I was away from the boundaries and consequences of real life. I was experiencing the gut lie men like to entertain, the same one ingenious marketers capitalize on when they whisper tag lines like, "What happens in Vegas stays in Vegas."

VENUS AND VEGAS

In their romantic lives most women intuitively search for a life-long committed relationship. Men search for adventure and variety. We know deep inside that a monogamous committed relationship will bring us the most joy in the long run. At least that's what we heard in church and in college Bible studies. But we still cast a glance; we still entertain fantasies; we still allow ourselves to be tempted by the lie that we can act out our dreams without consequences.

The book says women are from Venus and men are from Mars. I say, women *are* from Venus, but men are from Vegas.

One of the problems we men encounter is that we are prone to embracing two tasty lies:

1. We think there are no consequences to our behavior as long as no one knows.

- So what if I flirt with a woman at 35,000 feet?
- So what if I cross the line with that assistant at work, or the lady next door?
- So what if I cruise the Internet late at night?
- So what if I pursue some enticement on my business trips?

"What happens in Vegas stays in Vegas." Guys, let's just agree for starters: as nice as that sounds, it's a bald-faced lie, and we know it. There are many consequences to the pursuit of selfish enticement in secret:

- Thought-life defines our conscience
- Secrets destroy trust
- Compromise undermines relationship
- Hidden sin brings shame, and lots of it

No consequences to our behavior? Give me a break. We know better than that regardless of what we tell ourselves.

2. We think our sexual exploits, whether actual or virtual, will satisfy our deepest longings. They don't, they won't, and they can't. How many deeply fulfilled promiscuous men have you known? How many illicit affairs have you seen bring lasting joy?

Can we honestly say that the furtive trolling on Internet porn sites, or actual encounters with tragic young strippers or prostitutes selling their bodies and souls, brings an increased sense of character and respect into our lives rather than an abiding remorse and shame?

The evidence is undeniable; millions of men are trapped in the lie that the pursuit of sexual fulfillment through pornography will satisfy their unmet longings. Consider these 2015 stats from various sources:

- Porn sites receive more regular traffic than Netflix, Amazon, and Twitter combined each month. (HuffPost)
- 69% of the pay-per-view Internet content market is pornography. (Covenant Eyes)
- 9 out of 10 boys are exposed to pornography before the age of 18; the average age of first exposure is 11. (Covenant Eyes)
- 35% of all Internet downloads are porn-related. (WebRoot)
- 34% of Internet users have been exposed to unwanted porn via ads, pop-ups, etc. (WebRoot)
- 64% of Christian men say they watch porn at least once a month. (Covenant Eyes)
- 68% of young adult men use porn at least once every week. (Covenant Eyes)
- 75% of pastors don't make themselves accountable to anyone for their Internet use. (Covenant Eyes)

In my experience working with men on a heart level for many years, roughly 80% of men struggle with porn to a significant degree. An additional 10% are addicted to the extent that their pursuit of porn or illicit sex seriously harms them financially, relationally, and in the use of their time. The remaining 10% have unusual freedom, or they struggle with lying.

The evidence is overwhelming; enormous numbers of men are sexually unfulfilled and are a looking for relief outside of marriage. (Sadly, the numbers are growing rapidly for women, too.) What an awful, broken reflection this is on a gift that God intended for such beauty and depth.

Why is porn such an issue for men?

Because we are visually oriented and aroused, much more so than women.

Because we are by nature more prone to conquest and variety than to commitment.

Because the biological chemistry of arousal in men happens so suddenly.

All these factors provide a perfect "container" where the visual stimulation of an attractive woman, whether in the flesh, on paper, or on screen, causes an internal explosion that demands release. When this sequence is followed by the emotional and biological pleasure of an orgasm, it's a compelling combination. Especially if the woman never says "No," and especially if she requires no commitment!

How deeply the heavenly Creator must weep at this distortion of a sacred longing.

Strength and Beauty

Beryl and I once went to a Scottish festival in Estes Park, Colorado. It was a wonderful day of enjoying Scottish athletic competitions, marching bands in kilts, and traditional Irish dances, all nestled in a spectacular setting on a lake surrounded by mountains.

In the afternoon we went to see an Australian band named "Brother," which we had seen before in Breckenridge. They were incredibly cool. The band took the stage; five men in kilts, leather boots, bagpipes, rugged beards, drums, guitars, and a didgeridoo (an indigenous Aborigine wind instrument). The effect of the powerful mix of music was striking.

At some point during the concert I noticed three women in the front row across from where Beryl and I were sitting. They stood there staring at the band. They grinned, they took pictures, they held on to each, all while never losing sight of these men with names like Angus and Fergus.

I was struck by the sheer joy on the faces of these women, and by the way they seemed enraptured with the manly strength displayed on stage. Their reaction didn't look sexual to me; rather they looked enthralled. But you could see how easily it could lead to sexual sin. I suspect that if any of the guys in the band invited any of the women in the audience for some time alone, they would have had several takers.

About an hour later another band took the stage. This one was a family from Canada who played and sang lush Celtic songs. There was an amazing amount of talent for one family—the dad doing lead vocals, the mom on keyboard, a son on drums, another on guitar. But one person in particular stood out to me, and to every other man in the audience: the daughter.

She stood center stage playing the violin. She was strikingly beautiful as she swayed in time with the music. The effect of her amazing talent, physical beauty, and body flowing with the music was captivating. Everyone in the audience, especially the men, was enthralled. No doubt that's why she was center stage. They knew who the audience wanted to see.

Her performance wasn't at all sexual; on the contrary, it seemed pure and natural. But it was easy to see how "steamy" it could have been had her dress been more revealing, or had she emphasized her swaying movement.

The effect of these performances stood out to me in jarring contrast. Neither was sexual or sinful in their nature. Rather, each portrayed the powerful nature of masculinity in the first case, and femininity in the second. They reflected the different aspects God designed in each. Men emanate inner or outer strength; women emanate inner or outer beauty. In their purest form they aren't sinful, but they are absolutely enthralling and captivating. God designed that.

A THIRST TO DIE FOR

A few years ago I came across a quote that was so jarring and unexpected that it staggered me. I dropped the book and let the words sink in, and then literally exclaimed, "Whoa!" The amazing quote is most often attributed to British author and theologian, G.K. Chesterton: "Every man who knocks on the door of a brothel is looking for God."

In other words, every man who pursues fulfillment of his sexual desires with a prostitute is actually looking for a deeper relationship with God.

What?!

The more I thought on this, the more I realized it's true! Even more, that means that every man who pursues porn, an affair, an enticing flirtation at 35,000 feet is really looking for something spiritual. That doesn't remotely excuse this pursuit, but it does help explain it.

What is it about God that we men are looking for? Connection, relationship, to be known and accepted, a sense that we matter to someone, significance. These are God-given longings, but we look for their fulfillment in all the wrong places.

Have you noticed how frequently men will risk complete compromise of their values, their marriages, and their reputations to pursue a short-term, illegitimate enticement? Perhaps you saw the old TV show *To Catch a Predator* where a guy in a computer chat room thinks he's talking to a young teen. He and the girl arrange a meeting at her home, which he eventually enters, thinking he's fulfilling a secret fantasy.

What he doesn't realize is that the girl is actually a vice cop and the home is wired and filled with hidden cameras. The girl excuses herself and out from behind a wall pops the condescending host who interviews the horrified victim. The cameras roll. It makes for great TV. What an awful commentary on our culture this is.

The look of horrified shock and pending disaster on the face of the "perp" is awful! Most of them, after submitting to an interview, eventually run out of the house, thinking they've been released, only to be captured, wrestled to the ground, and arrested by cops waiting outside.

Unbelievably, many of the perpetrators have seen the show! Some even say, "I knew it was going to be you guys." Still, they show up. Like sheep stumbling dumbly toward slaughter, they move toward the irresistible lure of their fantasies.

Many of these men are the creeps we'd expect. But some are teachers or respectable businessmen. One is a youth pastor, another a rabbi. They are you and me. I want to weep for them, and I do.

We could go on and list all the politicians and church leaders who have made the same stunning career-ending choices, but we won't. They are easy targets. Low-hanging fruit. The point is, this pattern is everywhere.

What in the world compels them to risk losing everything—their reputations, their marriages, their self-esteem— to chase after a sexual fantasy? What compels us?

I've experienced lust and attraction to porn. Most men are in roughly the same boat. Some of us know it's an area of vulnerability we need to avoid, others have fallen victim to an addiction that consumes time, money, and character. We've had varying degrees of success in moving beyond temptation.

When I find myself falling into a pattern of straying eyes, I've tried discipline with some degree of success. I've tried wearing rubber bands on my wrist, snapping them every time I'm tempted to lust. I've brought other men into my life to let them know when I'm going to be in a vulnerable situation so I'm not alone.

But I don't only want short-term tactics. I don't want tricks that fade. I want to understand the deeper issues going on beneath the surface of this journey toward purity, and then I want to make wise choices.

What is at work in my heart? Why am I drawn to the beauty of women? Why do I want to turn it into selfish gratification? Why do the vast majority of men reading this sentence also struggle with this battle?

One of the longings God placed in the hearts of men, in addition to a longing for love, is the desire for respect and significance. As mentioned in a previous chapter, for most men this is their greatest longing, more so than love.

When we pursue sin, lust, porn, or an illicit relationship, one of the thirsts we are longing to quench is significance. What do we reap in pursuing those enticements? Self-respect? Of course not. What we reap is shame; the exact opposite of what we desire at our deepest level.

If we learn this from experience, why do we make repeated mistakes in pursuing short-term pleasure? Because the pleasure appears more attractive than the consequences. Proverbs 5:15–23 (*The Message*) describes a clear analogy of the initial enticement, and then sad consequence, of sexual sin:

Do you know the saying, "Drink from your own rain barrel,
draw water from your own spring-fed well?"
It's true. Otherwise, you may one day come home
and find your barrel empty and your well polluted.

Your spring water is for you and you only,
not to be passed around among strangers.
Bless your fresh-flowing fountain!
Enjoy the wife you married as a young man!
Lovely as an angel, beautiful as a rose—
don't ever quit taking delight in her body.
Never take her love for granted!
Why would you trade enduring intimacies for cheap thrills
with a whore?
for dalliance with a promiscuous stranger?

Mark well that God doesn't miss a move you make;
he's aware of every step you take.
The shadow of your sin will overtake you;
you'll find yourself stumbling all over yourself in the dark.
Death is the reward of an undisciplined life;
your foolish decisions trap you in a dead end.

The voice of wisdom in Proverbs urges us to be men who are faithful to our women and grateful for the wives God has given us. We may know the subtle temptation that speaks the lie: "You really deserve someone smarter, funnier, wealthier, prettier, thinner…" From this perspective perhaps it's clear how self-centered and foolish that kind of thinking is. This passage tells us never to "quit taking delight in" our wives. Any temporary "whore" (just quoting), whether virtual or real, is going to bring her own baggage.

Is there any doubt as to the consequences of pursuing short-term selfish gratification? "What happens in Vegas stays in Vegas?" Please.

SPIRITUAL THIRST, BROKEN CISTERNS

The source of what draws us to temptation is actually a God-designed thirst for beauty, pleasure, adventure, risk, and intimacy. It's all part of the hunger that God put in male hearts.

But we need to understand, this world is fallen and will never give these things to us in ways that fully satisfy us. The sad truth is that because creation itself and everything in it is under the curse of the Fall, *nothing* this side of heaven and eternal intimacy with God will *ever* fully satisfy the longings we wrestle with.

Even the best of marriages leaves a sacred gap between our God-given thirst and a woman's ability to fully quench that thirst. Our challenge is to accept that, to pursue legitimate sources of fulfillment, and to reject cheap substitutes.

Far too often we have chosen false sources of satisfaction. Jeremiah 2:12–13 speaks directly to this pattern:

"Be appalled at this, you heavens,
 and shudder with great horror,"
declares the LORD.
   "My people have committed two sins:
They have forsaken me,
the spring of living water,
and have dug their own cisterns,
broken cisterns that cannot hold water."

When men (or women) pursue lust, pornography, sex chat rooms, or promiscuous relationships, all of them figuratively or literally the door of a brothel, these verses tell us we're making two mistakes:

1. We forsake God himself: Although he is the true source of the living water that quenches our deepest thirst, we essentially say, "God, you are not really enough for me. I'm going another direction."

2. We dig broken cisterns: We pretend that our own solutions will truly satisfy. They can't. They are man-made, so they can't quench spiritual thirst. Beyond that, they leak.

Men, we must see the bigger story that is taking place in our hearts. We thirst for something God-given, which can only be God-quenched. When we doubt that he is truly enough we look for our own shallow sources of satisfaction. We dig our own cisterns.

We stagger into the girl's home; we click on the next link; we pursue the enticing flirtation at work; we linger on the figure of the woman strolling through the restaurant.

In every case we are knocking on the door of a brothel in our search for deeper intimacy with God. None of these choices will ever satisfy on a long-term basis. If we choose a pattern of pursuing these "broken cisterns" they will ultimately bring great horror. Some of you reading these words can personally attest to that horror.

Oswald Chambers states in his book, *My Utmost for His Highest*: "There is only One Being who can satisfy the last aching abyss of the human heart, and that is the Lord Jesus Christ." C.S. Lewis echoes the same refrain in *Mere Christianity*: "God cannot give us happiness and peace apart from Himself. It is not there. There is no such thing."

"Every man who knocks on the door of a brothel is looking for God." To that I would add, every man who *digs his own broken cisterns* is also looking for God—in himself. We deceive ourselves into thinking we can solve a spiritual problem with an earthly solution of our own design. In doing so we deny God and worship our own intellect or creativity.

Men, we already know the broken cisterns we look to won't quench the thirst. That's why we keep looking for a bigger and deeper well. There is only one "spring of living water." It's a deep relationship with God through his Son, Jesus Christ, who made it clear, "If anyone is thirsty, let him come to me and drink...I am the way and the truth and the life. No one comes to the Father except through me...seek and you will find." (John 7:37; 14:6; Matthew 7:7)

First Corinthians 6:18 says to, "Flee from sexual immorality. All other sins a person commits are outside the body, but whoever sins sexually, sins against their own body." The consequences of these choices are not only physical and relational, but they unleash a new cycle of shame into our lives. Guaranteed.

God knows how he designed us and he warns us throughout Scripture to stay away from promiscuity. In the end it kills. We think it brings satisfaction of our longings for respect, adventure, and intimacy when in reality it brings shame and guilt, which kill the heart.

COURAGEOUS CHOICES

A committed, faithful relationship with one woman is the most profound human relationship most of us men will ever experience. But even when our wives can't give us all we long for, we have no excuse for making choices that break their hearts and harm our own souls. Rather, a truly courageous, strong, and godly man does four things:

1. He remembers who he is in God's eyes. He is a temple in which the Spirit resides. God urges us to keep it clean and holy for his sake.

2. He recognizes his longings are deeper than for the mere thrill of enticing images, and the momentary excitement of allowing his eyes and his mind to wander. His true longings are for adventure, beauty, joy, significance, intimacy, and respect. These are manly desires.

3. When these longings are not fulfilled, he disciplines himself to avoid the circumstances and environments that entice him. A hallmark of manly strength and trustworthiness is the ability to say "No" to longings we know offer short-term pleasure but longer-term regret. This may mean we say:

- NO to going to the gym with the late-afternoon beauties, and instead hang out with the early-morning grizzly gym rats.
- NO to traveling alone or with a female partner.
- NO to keeping our itinerary and points of temptation a secret from others.
- NO to Internet exploration, even before we start up the computer.

Saying no leaves a momentary emptiness, but it's what a man does for the benefit of his heart and the well-being of those he loves.

4. He takes his emptiness to the Father: The Creator gave men the deep desire for significance, for respect, and for intimacy. Mature men know this broken world will never entirely fulfill those longings. It's only by truly trusting the Father that we can experience a deeper level of intimacy and significance that porn will never provide.

We must understand that the life-giving way to pursue longing is to fill emptiness with righteousness. The apostle Paul writes:

> Summing it all up, friends, I'd say you'll do best by filling your
> minds and meditating on things true, noble, reputable, authen-
> tic, compelling, gracious—the best, not the worst; the beauti-
> ful, not the ugly; things to praise, not things to curse. Put into
> practice what you learned from me, what you heard and saw
> and realized. Do that, and God, who makes everything work
> together, will work you into his most excellent harmonies.
> (Philippians 4:8 *The Message*)

In closing, allow me to recommend the best book I've ever read on
the subjects of sexual temptation and the pursuit of purity. It's entitled
Surfing for God: Discovering the Divine Desire Beneath Sexual Struggle
by Michael Cusick. The first time I saw the title I noticed Cusick's
reference to "surfing" the Internet and that he connected it to a search
for God. I was sure he must be referencing Chesterton's quote. Indeed
he is. Cusick's honesty and insight into this journey, that's so familiar
to so many men, is superb.

QUESTIONS
FOR FURTHER THOUGHT OR DISCUSSION

1. Do you have any recollection of your dad using, hiding or showing
   you pornography? If so, what were the circumstances?

2. When was your first exposure to porn? What response did it bring
   up for you?

3. On a scale of 1-10—"1" being it rarely draws your attention, "10"
   being it's a significant daily battle—how would you rank your vulnerability to porn (or illicit sex)?

4. G. K. Chesterton says, "Every man who knocks on the door of a
   brothel is looking for God." How would you re-state this in your

own words? In other words, while you may not stand outside a brothel, what doorway to temptation do you return to?

5. If you ranked porn low on the scale above (1-3), is there another false idol or unsatisfied source of longing in your life that you know pulls too much energy from you? What is it?

6. How do we live with, or satisfy in a healthy way, the unmet longings we all have?

PART II
IDENTITY

CHAPTER 4

WARRIOR: STRENGTH MOTIVATED BY COURAGE

Not long ago I sat in a room with about 40 men spanning the ages of 18 to 49. When I asked them, "What does it mean to be a man?" they sat in silent discomfort. Some eventually offered vague descriptions like, "He's strong," or "He wears the pants in the family," or "He's the one who shaves."

What does it mean to be a man? Many of us have no clue.

That question was rarely asked 100 years ago. For centuries, men passed on their traditions and wisdom about manhood from generation to generation. Fathers taught their sons by example and often extended this teaching into training for a vocation. Sons would grow under the teaching of their fathers and would often pursue the same career. Jesus is an example of this in that he was trained in carpentry, which was the same vocation as his earthly father, Joseph.

During childhood, a boy would often be most influenced by his mother. She would love him, care for him, protect and provide for him in the tenderhearted and deeply committed way almost all mothers do. But in many pre-modern cultures when the son reached the age of maturity, usually at puberty—around 13 or 14—his father would take over as the main influence in his life. This often began with the recognition that the son had reached a point where he was entering manhood. The men of the village would come together to call their sons out from the mothers and into the company of other men.

At this point a number of rituals or experiences marked the beginning of this training. These rituals usually had a symbolic meaning that pointed the son to the new responsibility of becoming a man. These might include some physical challenge such as going into the forest alone to hunt a wild animal. Another common experience was for the son to go off alone without food with the challenge of creating a vision or sense of mission for his life.

As Western culture developed in the industrial age, these rites of passage had more to do with a son's apprenticeship in his father's skill, such as tailoring, farming, or coal mining. The mastering of these tasks demonstrated that the son was a man and could assume the responsibilities of manhood. The other men in the community celebrated and affirmed this new man.

For these young men, what it meant to be a man was very clear. A man's identity was shaped by a constant definition of manhood for that community. Young men followed the lead of older men. There was little questioning of this process.

Today we have largely lost these formal traditions of initiation. Instead, even adult men are confused about what it means to be a true man, and they don't know how to guide their sons in a clear way to achieve manhood.

As a result we rely on a variety of informal "rites of passage" to convince our boys they are men. Depending on where boys live, at 16, 18 or 21, they can drive a car, join the army, vote, and buy tobacco, alcohol, weapons, and pornography. Some of these rites demand genuine maturity; some of them are harmful. Some boys may be ready to make these choices; many aren't. Too often our society does little to ensure they are prepared for these kinds of responsibilities. Instead, the culture simply offers "rights" based solely on age.

Over a lifetime, boys without direction and guidance become men who hide doubts that they measure up to manhood. They live with a subtle doubt that "they have what it takes to be a man" (whatever *that* is.) If they become fathers, they have little idea of what exactly to pass on to their sons.

What does it mean to be a man? We can get a clear idea of what Jesus thought by examining his response to a very difficult question directed to him by a teacher of the law. "Of all the commandments, which is the most important?" (Mark 12:28). Jesus said simply, "Love the Lord your God with all your heart with all your soul and with all your mind and with all your strength…love your neighbor as yourself" (vv. 30–31).

In two sentences he not only fully answered a spiritual riddle thrown at him, he revealed how God has designed men and women: with heart (emotions), soul (spirit), mind (intellect) and strength (body). That covers everything; there isn't anything else about us other than these four aspects. In this and the next three chapters we will look at these qualities and discover how they come to life in genuine men.

Women, of course, have the same four components, but they live them out differently than men do. This is because God has designed men and women distinctly. This is one of the most mysterious, attractive, and sacred qualities of how God has designed us.

The book of Genesis says that women and men are both made "in his image," but each gender demonstrates a different attribute of who God is in his full person. Neither men nor women are superior; we both wonderfully embody God's design. But we reveal different aspects of who he is, his nature. For the purposes of this book, we will look solely at male qualities.

I see a corresponding characteristic for each of the four components referred to in Mark 12:30 that defines godly manhood: Compassion, Confidence, Conviction, and Courage. I also find it helpful to picture a corresponding image that illustrates the various roles men live out: Lover, King, Mentor, and Warrior.

Here are the correlations as I see them:

Heart – Compassion – Lover
Soul – Confidence – King
Mind – Conviction – Mentor
Strength – Courage – Warrior

These components are empowered by a commitment to living in a way that honors God and benefits others. Men who are growing in each of these areas are truly noble men.

As I speak to men on these topics I notice a quizzical confusion, and even resistance, about how compassion can be manly—along with an intuitive acceptance that courage definitely is. So, I like entering this journey through the "courage door." Let's start with that one first. But be ready. Compassion will come immediately afterward.

One more important point to be watching for: each of these four components can take either a Noble quality in our lives or a Shadow quality. The Noble quality directs the innate God-designed power of that component toward the benefit of others. It's other-centered.

The Shadow quality has the same power and strength that God gives all men, but its intention is for a man's own benefit, not others'. The action is self-absorbed.

You'll recognize these qualities very quickly. The distinctions are in men all around us. They may also appear in our own mirrors.

STRENGTH: THE COURAGE OF A WARRIOR

What was the time when you were the most frightened in your life?

For me it was in 1978, at the height of the Cold War, at 1 a.m. on a dark, heavily forested, lonely road outside Budapest, Hungary, when I nearly drove into a sentry standing in the middle of the road.

There were two reasons I was frightened: I was smuggling about 2,000 Bibles superficially hidden in plastic garbage bags just behind the front seat of my van. And the soldier eventually had his face at my open window, my passport in one hand, an AK-47 pointed at my head, his finger on the trigger and alcohol on his breath. It was not a welcome combination of circumstances.

I had made a horribly wrong turn looking for a campsite to hide out overnight before delivering the literature to a pastor. After taking my passport, the sentry insisted I follow him alone into the forest on foot.

I left Beryl in the front seat with these instructions: "I don't know where he's taking me, but if I'm not back in one hour, go to the campsite (she now knew it was the opposite fork in the road than the one I'd taken) and stay there overnight. I'll meet you at the train station in downtown Budapest at 6 a.m. If I'm not there, leave everything, the Bibles and van, and get the first train to Austria because I'll have been arrested."

As it turned out, the sentry took me to his tiny, well-hidden outpost in the forest, and only wanted a bribe to return my passport. He was too drunk to think about searching the van and I was more than happy to pay him the equivalent of 50 cents to get out of there as fast as I could. I shuddered with fear throughout the whole incident.

Beryl and I experienced significant fear, but there were two factors that motivated us: We fought for the courageous Eastern European Christians who literally put their lives at risk to receive the literature we brought them. And we fought for the principle stated in Scripture when Jesus said, "I will build my church, and the gates of [hell] will not overcome it" (Matthew 16:18).

As I look back at that eventful evening I had good reason to be scared.

Nor was that the last time I wrestled with fear. Far from it.

There is a foolish way in which men are told to have "No Fear," as if saying so makes it true. Maybe if we say it louder. Maybe we should get a bigger bumper sticker or cap that brags, not quite convincingly, No Fear!

Men, let's be honest: fear exists. There are times that fear is the only normal response to the threats, confusion, or uncertainty we encounter in life. Those who claim to never feel fear are either liars or are fooling only themselves.

The world often teaches the false belief that men should have no fear. The truth is closer to the opposite; fear is at the very heart of courage. Courage is not the absence of fear; courage is the willingness to step toward what we fear. I'd go so far as to say courage doesn't exist without fear.

I don't think fear is a sin. How can it be? Fear is one of the normal emotions God has given us, often for our own protection and safety. We know what it feels like and we know what kind of conditions bring it creeping to the surface, or digging at our insides. Fear is a physiological response that we can hardly stop from happening. Fear alone is not sin.

It's how we respond to fear that determines its ultimate impact. Does fear paralyze us with doubt and passivity? Does it cause us to ignore God's ability to guide us through a dark valley to the other side? If so, it becomes a reflection of our fallenness from God's design and intention for us as men.

Or does fear compel us to take action, despite uncertainty? Does it instill in us a willingness to move ahead trusting in God's sovereignty? If so, it becomes powerful evidence of one of the main qualities God put in the hearts of men: an orientation toward movement and action, even when we feel personal risk.

Here's the first image of what godly manhood looks like: *When we love God, and others, with all our strength, we have the courage of a warrior.*

SHADOW WARRIORS

There are worldly Shadow Warriors in our lives and there are godly Noble Warriors. When I was in high school, I had a summer job as a lifeguard at the local swimming pool. One evening I kicked a kid out of the pool for doing "splash-dives" (cannon balls, can-openers, etc.) which, as fun as they were, were not allowed in our pools.

It turned out he was the wrong guy to mess with. I had seen him at school; he was what we called a "greaser." Sorry, but we weren't very PC back then. He and his buddies wore black leather jackets, slicked-back hair, pointed-toe black Beatle boots, and white "Dago Ts" (at least we didn't call them "wife-beaters" as I've heard my sons describe them).

He and his scary buddies had a reputation for short tempers, sharp knives, and quick fists. I didn't possess any of those. As I thumbed him out of the pool, he slowly walked by me and snarled, "I'm waiting for you." Those were some of the most frightening words I'd heard in my life to that point.

For the next hour, until closing, I kept my eye on the outer fence. Sure enough, there he was on patrol, biding his time, waiting for his chance at revenge.

As luck would have it, I was the guard responsible for closing up. It was my responsibility to take one last walk around the darkened pool and locker rooms to ensure no bodies were floating on the surface and the facility was empty. Every step of the way, I trembled as I watched this frightening fighter at his post outside the fence, waiting patiently.

Finally, there was no avoiding my fate. I turned out the last lights and walked out of the door, and there he was, in all his black-leather glory. He planted himself about ten feet from me, swearing, explaining what was going to happen to my face, clenching and unclenching his fists. I saw no knife. Yet.

I feared for my life in the presence of this imposing alpha male who bristled with a bravado and confidence I knew nothing of. I was not going to take the first swing, that was certain; but I decided I wasn't going to run. I would face the judgment to come and hope to survive.

Suddenly, my younger brother, Clyde, came around the corner about 20 feet away. He and my dad had just pulled into the parking lot to take me home. You might think that I'd call him over, in relief, knowing that two on one would give me a better chance against my foe.

But that's not how I responded. I turned to Clyde and, with tears welling up in my eyes (the same way they are now as I write this), yelled, "Get out! Get out of here! Now!" Clyde stood paralyzed with shock at what he was seeing and hearing, slowly turned, and disappeared around the corner again. Once again, I faced my tormentor alone.

Just as suddenly, another figure appeared, Mr. Mann, the pool manager and a wrestling coach at the high school. I had no idea he was still there, but he walked out of the building, stared at us, and said, "What's this?" Neither the greaser nor I said a word. But Mr. Mann could tell what was going on. He turned his bulk toward my nemesis and threatened, "Get the hell out of here, or I'll kick your ass!" With a moment's hesitation, then resignation, he turned and left. I was saved.

As I rode home with my dad and Clyde, it was all I could do to hold in my tears of fear and shame. Dad asked me to tell him what happened. But there was no relating the story. I could barely speak. And I didn't want him to know what a weak son he had.

In retrospect, I realized that it was that same shame over my seeming lack of courage and confidence that caused me to lash out at Clyde. I didn't want my younger brother to watch me get beaten, to see me weak and afraid. I'd literally take a beating before allowing him to see me weak.

Shadow Warriors are those men who use their evident power for their own benefit. Their primary battle is to fight for self and they will use any advantage they have in strength or intimidation to assert themselves. The world gives us many examples of these kinds of men:

- Political leaders who abuse or imprison their citizens
- Businessmen who ignore integrity to cheat their own employees out of their retirement funds
- Church leaders who use their position of authority to harm, shame, or control those who trust them
- Men who assert physical strength in order to harrass, intimidate or assault women
- Movie thugs, wrestling posers, and arrogant sports figures whose primary goal is to dominate and embarrass others by drawing attention to their own abilities

These are, indeed, Shadow Warriors. These are the men we see who stalk the pool, pose in the end zone, intimidate in the boardroom, or strut on the rock stage. More often than not their bravado masks a wounded heart that is deeply insecure and uncertain of its own value. They pose and power-up to impress others with an external façade because deep inside they have a nagging doubt that they truly matter.

NOBLE WARRIORS

Noble Warriors take the opposite path. They marshal their courage, even in the face of fear, to fight for others, not themselves. They fight on behalf of people they love and principles they believe in. Noble Warriors stand up for something bigger than themselves and are even willing to put themselves at risk to defend what they believe in.

A principle to remember for men of courage is: *They get in the way.*

When Eve was threatened and confused in the Garden, she needed Adam to step up, speak up, and get in the way, to stand between her and the threat. Instead, he remained silent and passive and simply watched what unfolded in front of him.

Men have unfortunately behaved this same way ever since. Far too often men allow fear to paralyze them into silence and passivity. To me, these two, silence and passivity, are the original male sins.

When men see co-workers being mistreated, they need to get in the way and speak up for fairness. When dads see their children being misled by the values of the world, they need to get in the way and speak truth. When boys watch a friend being teased or bullied at school, they need to get in the way and stand up for those who are weaker or outnumbered.

Not long ago a friend of mine, whom I'll call Ross, was visiting Turkey. He and a couple of tourist colleagues came upon a young man of less-than-average height being yelled at by a group of larger men. Ross, who stands no more than 5'8" himself, didn't know what the argument was about but his heart immediately went out to the smaller man outnumbered by a group of street thugs.

At first the abuse toward the smaller man was verbal and clearly demeaning, but then it became physical as the men shoved him to the ground. Something deep inside Ross suddenly kicked in. It was something unidentifiable and it didn't make rational sense. He moved toward the man on the ground and got in the way between him and the bullies. Perhaps he identified with the size of the smaller guy. Perhaps he rose up against the injustice of several big guys picking on one man.

Whatever the case, Ross took action and walked into fear. He didn't think and he didn't ignore what he was feeling. He stepped in front of the smaller man, faced the group of bullies, shoved the biggest guy in the chest, and, with all the fierceness he could muster, demanded at the top of his voice that they leave the helpless man alone.

The men were so shocked at his boldness (regardless of whether they understood his English), so surprised that someone would stand up for a stranger, that they muttered, spat out a few insults, and walked away. People know a Noble Warrior when they see one. They fight for people they love and principles they believe in.

In this case, Ross was not fighting for someone he loved; he didn't even know the victim. He was fighting for a principle he believed in—justice. He simply would not allow injustice to be committed right in front of him.

BIBLICAL WARRIORS

The Bible gives us several examples of warriors. David was a shepherd, a poet, a musician and, to the shock of the intimidating Philistines, a warrior. He had a great conviction that his cause was right, that God was behind it, and that God would strengthen him.

David boldly stood before Goliath, who was far bigger than he was, and brought him to the ground with one well-placed stone fired from a sling. It was courage that allowed him to face his fear and step toward a literal giant in his life.

Joshua was another Old Testament man who defined the image of a biblical warrior. Over and over again God used Joshua to defeat the enemies of Israel and lead them across the Jordan River into the Promised Land. We might think Joshua was fearless and never encountered any doubt as to whether God was with him or would deliver him from threats he faced. But I don't think that's the case.

The first chapter of the book of Joshua relates an inspiring challenge to Joshua in which God repeated one exhortation more than any other: "Be strong and courageous" (v. 6). "Be strong and very courageous" (v. 7). "Be strong and courageous. Do not be afraid; do not be discouraged" (v. 9).

Even Joshua's followers chimed in: "Only be strong and courageous!" (v. 18).

Could it be that God gave Joshua this message because he didn't feel at all strong and courageous? The Lord could have said, "Joshua, be faithful and righteous," or, "Joshua, be kind and compassionate." But he didn't. I believe he gave Joshua the message he most needed to hear: "Go. I'm with you. Be strong and courageous."

And with that encouragement Joshua stepped into uncertainty, threat, and perhaps fear, and led the Israelites into a land full of blessing and promise.

When we encounter uncertainty because of job loss, threat because of conflict, or fear due to resistance we are afraid to engage, we can learn from Joshua's example. Trust God, be strong and courageous, and step into fear.

It's one thing to refer to fighting warriors from the Old Testament. What about Jesus; was he a warrior? We can answer that question by reviewing the definition of a Noble Warrior: he is a man who fights on behalf of people he loves and principles he believes in. Jesus did this regularly, and he ended up dying because of it.

Jesus demonstrated his courage when he drove the moneychangers out of the temple (Matthew 21:12–13). He was so profoundly disturbed and convicted that he stood up for the purity of the temple, a principle he deeply believed in. He employed righteous anger in a healthy way to oppose wrong behavior.

Jesus was certainly a warrior when he cleared the temple of thieves, but he was a warrior in even more profound ways:

- When he stood in front of an angry mob and defended the woman they were about to stone; he got in the way
- When he endured enormous agony alone in the Garden of Gethsemane
- When he willingly submitted to beating and whipping
- When he submitted to being nailed to the cross, thereby defeating death for all of us

UNSEEN ENEMY

Our encounters with conflict are certainly not as epic as the ones Jesus faced. Nevertheless, men who long to be more Christ-like will absolutely face resistance and temptation. Ultimately we know that the toughest battles we will ever fight are against an unseen enemy.

Ephesians 6:10–12 tells us that our battle is not against flesh and blood, but against spiritual powers that harm our heart, soul, mind, and strength. This Enemy looks for anyone he can harm and destroy. "Your enemy the devil prowls around like a roaring lion looking for someone to devour" (1 Peter 5:8).

In this spiritual battle we must draw our courage and strength from the Holy Spirit who lives in us. We need to pay attention to what challenges and trials are hiding beneath the surface of the fear we face:

- If I'm afraid of being demeaned, what is the spiritual lesson for me? My value rests in the love and acceptance of the One whose opinion actually matters the most—God, who created me.
- If I'm afraid of failing, what biblical principle can give me courage? God can accomplish his purposes in my life (spiritual transformation) even when I am weak.
- If I'm afraid of being left alone, what would God say to me in response? "I am always with you. I will never leave you alone."

The deepest longing most men have is to be respected by others. As a result the most common fear we experience is fear of failure—the loss of respect from others. The greatest source of courage when we feel fear of failure is to be convinced that our significance is not defined by success in the eyes of the world nor even in the opinions of other Christians. Our significance is established by our Creator who intentionally knit us together is our mothers' wombs (Psalm 139:13).

We want to be well-liked and respected by others; that's natural. But others do not determine our value and significance unless we grant them that power. Our value is determined by God who designed us on purpose, and by his Son who gave himself for us. These two truths can be the foundation of courage in the face of fear from spiritual battles like self-condemnation and shame, or human battles, like being demeaned by a person in authority.

Young men of courage resist the pressure of friends who want them to use drugs or go after sex in order to be accepted. Rather than giving in to the temptation to bully another student, they stand by the side of those being bullied. They have a toughness that allows them to stand strong and defend what they believe in.

Older men of courage take a similar stand when tempted to compromise their integrity, treat a fellow employee unfairly, or cut corners to make more money. They are able to resist pressure and stand firmly on behalf of others they care about, and on behalf of principles they will not compromise.

Truly courageous men do not give in to the temptation of silence or passivity. They are defined by a willingness to step forward, to take action, even if they might fail. They have a strength that comes from within, rather than the bluster and posing demonstrated by those whose primary motivation is anger or self-doubt.

THE MAN IN THE ARENA

President Teddy Roosevelt was known as a man of action and, indeed, a warrior. Many times his courageous actions led to praise; other times he was the subject of great criticism. He made his opinion of his accusers clear when he gave a speech in Paris in 1910, which included the following comments:

> It is not the critic who counts; not the man who points out how the strong man stumbles, or where the doer of deeds could have done them better. The credit belongs to the man who is actually in the arena, whose face is marred by dust and sweat and blood; who strives valiantly; who errs, who comes short again and again, because there is no effort without error and shortcoming; but who does actually strive to do the deeds; who knows great enthusiasms, the great devotions; who spends himself in a worthy cause; who at the best knows in the end the triumph of high achievement, and who at the worst, if he fails, at least fails while daring greatly, so that his place shall never be with those cold and timid souls who neither know victory nor defeat.

Men, I want you to know that feeling fear is a part of life. But standing on the sidelines and not acting, or criticizing those who do act, is a demonstration of cowardice. The first man, Adam, stood on the sidelines when Eve needed him to get in the way. He failed her badly.

Courage is the willingness to step up; to encounter uncertainty; to risk failure, criticism, and embarrassment; to enter fear on behalf of people we love and principles we are willing to fight for—or even die for.

Are you the kind of man who will dare to step into the arena? Will you come forward when a person you care about needs you? Will you take action despite criticism when a person with less integrity is ignoring a principle you believe in? Will you speak up? These are the signs of a man of courage.

"Then I heard the voice of the Lord saying, 'Whom shall I send? And who will go for us?' And I said, 'Here am I. Send me!'" (Isaiah 6:8).

The world needs noble men who have the courage of a warrior. This quality is in you because God made you a man. Unleash it.

QUESTIONS
FOR FURTHER THOUGHT OR DISCUSSION

1. What is one of the most courageous things you've done? How did it require courage?

2. Have you ever met, lived with, or worked for a Shadow Warrior— someone who uses their strength primarily for their own benefit? Who was (s)he? How did (s)he intimidate you?

3. Who or what in your life currently creates the most fear in you? What next healthy step in addressing this fear would require the most courage from you?

4. Who is someone you have put yourself at risk for? How do you do that?

5. Can you think of principles or values you are willing to fight for? What are they?

CHAPTER 5

LOVER: A HEART MOVED BY COMPASSION

C ompassion is a word that's not often associated with manliness. It tends to bring up images of softness or tenderness that we may attribute more to femininity than to masculinity. If the subject comes up at men's retreats many feel a certain queasiness, suspecting that at some point they are going to have to cry and get all "touchy-feely." The idea of compassion may evoke the same response in us.

I agree. This isn't a very attractive picture of what men can expect at a retreat. But I disagree with the assumption that compassion is gooey and unmanly. My conviction is the opposite; compassion in a man is one of the most appealing and powerful qualities we can possess.

Compassion speaks of the ability of a man to get out of his head and into his heart. And the heart is where enormous strength and energy resides.

TWO HAND GESTURES

I've been a man long enough, and I've worked with men for long enough, that I know there are two invisible arm gestures going on as I get to know them, relate to them, or invite them to engage in an event or friendship:

- One hand is upward facing himself, with two fingers raised, drawing them repeatedly toward his face. It communicates, "Notice me. See me. Include me. Invite me."

- The other hand is directly between this first hand and my face. It, too, is pointed upward, but the palm is straight at me, fingers spread like a wall. It communicates, "Back off. What do you want? What are you up to? Get the heck outta my face."

Some say the longest foot in the world is the 12 inches from a man's head to his heart. The stereotype is often true; men tend to be more rational and aware of thought processes than emotional and aware of feelings. Sure, there are exceptions, but that's generally what they are: exceptions. However, when a man is able to really connect with, and act upon, what's going on deep inside his chest, he can become a force for enormous good and for the blessing of others.

Most of us grew up in a culture that expected boys to hide feelings and cover up any signs of fear or pain, which were considered unmanly. "Don't be such a baby. Big boys don't cry. Wipe that tear out of your eye."

These are actual words many of us heard growing up. The implied message was "Don't you dare show feelings; they're a sign of weakness." Those feelings are still there, of course. What do you think happens to them? They don't get expressed so they don't get healed; they get buried. Then a year or two—or 40—later they explode in a volcano of inexplicable rage completely out of proportion to the incident that brought them to the surface. That's because the feelings were submerged, left to fester, until the lid blew off under high pressure.

GIFT FROM GOD

Feelings (emotions) are given to us by God to help us be more aware of life and how we relate to others. Although we often learn to suppress them, all men have emotions. One way to remember some basic ones is with the acronym SASHET: Sad, Angry, Scared, Happy, Excited, Tender. Men, those are feelings.

There are many others, of course, but for starters these are some common emotions that men and women feel. Women just happen to do a better job of connecting to them and sharing them with others than men do. Perhaps you've heard the statement, "Women rapport, men report." It's largely true. Women have an ability to relate, connect, and share with each other in an intuitive way. Get men together and they exchange information: where we live, what we do, and what team we cheer for.

Most women feel emotions more easily than most men, and culture has frequently reinforced assumptions that exaggerate that effect. The truth is emotions are a gift from God to both genders. They allow us to go to a deeper level of understanding and connection with others. They help us comfort, encourage, cheer, grieve, inspire, and live for others—and to receive the same from them.

When we men cut ourselves off from our emotions because we believe they make us appear weak we actually cut ourselves off from people. We can't give love and we can't receive it. Instead, we may build walls of indifference to the feelings of others. In fact, we often wall off our own hearts.

SMELLING SMOKE

I once met a businessman for the first time for some spiritual mentoring. As he walked into the coffee shop I noticed his immaculately pressed suit, his shining black shoes, the perfectly executed Windsor knot in his tie, the crease in his pants that you could cut your finger on, and the part in his hair that looked like it was laid down with a straight-edge ruler. He made a perfect presentation.

As we got to know each other he focused on his academic and business accomplishments. They were impressive. Asking him more about his family and life story, I sensed resistance on his part to get too deep. He skipped over aspects of connection or memories that usually come to the surface with many men.

I definitely felt an imaginary straight-arm pressing into my chest lest I get too close. My reaction, of course, was to press in anyway.

As we closed our first session, I mentioned that the next time we met I'd like to start by hearing about his relationship with his dad.

"Oh, that's easy," he smirked. "We won't need much time for that."

Surprised, because to me father-son connections are of enormous importance, I asked, "Really? Why is that?"

"Never knew the guy," he said flippantly, as if it had no bearing on his story or on who he was.

Well, in fact, it had enormous bearing. Not surprisingly I learned that the abandonment he experienced from the man who gave him life was a huge factor in his commitment to presenting himself to others as impressively as possible.

I often hear comments from men similar to this man's. Their words imply, "Hey, that pain, that loss, happened a very long time ago. I've moved on. It doesn't matter anymore."

Yes, friend, it does matter. I sometimes tell these men it's as if their present life is a house they have built over the years. It has a foundation, of course, but they pay most attention to the façade, the "street view," and the neighborhood.

What they ignore is that when the foundation was laid, the concrete developed an enormous crack. Then the joists and cross beams were laid on top, sealing it off. Then one day there was a fire at this basement level. It smoldered and was eventually put out, but never repaired or replaced.

As the rest of the house was built, floor on top of impressive floor, the cracks and embers in the foundation remained sealed off. Over the years the home improvements focused on the siding, the paint, the roof, and the landscaping.

The man living in this house may make a good initial presentation. But as others get to know him, while they may not know the details of the damage in the foundation, they can smell the smoke.

Men whose story smells like smoke often have a disconnect between their heads and hearts. That disconnect prevents them from feeling emotions and from demonstrating compassion.

The word "compassion" starts with the prefix "com" meaning together or with. It's used in words like community and communication. The root word is "passion," which we associate with energy or strong feelings. Both of these are accurate meanings for passion, but not the deepest. At its heart the word "passion" means "suffering."

We hear it used this way at Easter when Passion Plays recount the agony of Jesus in the Garden of Gethsemane as he faced the cross. We saw it several years ago in the title of the Mel Gibson movie *The Passion of the Christ*, portraying the suffering of Jesus.

THE COMPASSION OF A LOVER

A man of compassion has the gift of not only feeling emotions, he is also able to experience the feelings and emotions of others and connect with them. Not only that, he is able to feel sad, afraid, angry, hurt, or happy in situations that trigger these feelings, and then let the right people know at the right time what he's going through. He is not ashamed of these feelings but knows they allow him to be completely aware of what's going on in his heart and in the hearts of others.

Second Corinthians 1:3–7 tells us how compassion works:

Praise be to the God and Father of our Lord Jesus Christ, the Father of compassion and the God of all comfort, who comforts us in all our troubles, so that we can comfort those in any trouble with the comfort we ourselves receive from God.

For just as we share abundantly in the sufferings of Christ, so also our comfort abounds through Christ. If we are distressed, it is for your comfort and salvation; if we are comforted, it is for your comfort, which produces in you patient endurance of the same sufferings we suffer. And our hope for you is firm, because we know that just as you share in our sufferings, so also you share in our comfort.

There is one phrase, and one word, in particular that stand out to me in this passage.

The phrase: *Father of compassion.* God, the Father, has authority over all compassion; he created it and is in charge of its presence on earth.

The word: *Comfort.* Do you notice how many times this word keeps reappearing? Nine times in five verses. Our ability to lend a hand, to come to the rescue, to bring a degree of hope into the lives of those who suffer—in short, to act heroically—is the result of compassion.

Compassion is not squishy. It's noble, it's powerful, and it's heroic.

Shadow Lovers

When I was a young man I was deeply concerned with other people's opinions of me. I believed the lie that others determined my value. Everyone was watching my behavior and performance and they were assigning grades. Believing that, I gave others the power to control my actions and feelings. I was committed to protecting my reputation by covering up my emotions, particularly those that looked weak or sinful.

Although I suspected I was pretty similar to most guys, in reality I thought I felt things on a deeper level than most. I didn't know if that was actually the case, but I sure didn't want to conduct a poll. I preferred to keep embarrassing or unpleasant feelings to myself.

Over the years I encountered all sorts of disappointment, loss, rejection, and shame, just like everyone else does. Those experiences began to change my inability, or my reluctance, to reveal myself to others. Slowly.

When Beryl and I fell in love in college in 1972, we fell fast and hard. We used to sit in the dining hall, staring dreamily across the room into one another's eyes, smiling. I know, it sounds obnoxious. Like I said, we fell fast and hard.

We dated regularly and had the kind of normal fun, conversations, storytelling, making out (just being honest) that most students did. We were in love and I thought everything was moving ahead as planned.

Until the night when we sat in the car at Beryl's dormitory parking lot after a date and, with tears in her eyes, she said, "I think we've hit a wall in our relationship." I looked tenderly into her welling eyes and said, "Huh?"

That led to a risky, honest, and ultimately crucial conversation where Beryl told me she felt like I had an emotional wall up that she couldn't get through. If we were going to go further in our relationship, I needed to let her in deeper than I had. Deeply shaken, I decided I would, and that made all the difference in our relationship.

This wasn't the last comment along those lines I heard out of the blue. During the 1980s a consultant spent some time with the mission organization I worked for. His task was to determine what the staff needs were and whether we had the right people in the right slots. I don't remember much of our first contact with each other, but my guess is that I was professional, collegial, reserved—and hidden.

Years later, after we became very good friends, he informed me over a meal, "Craig, when I first met you I respected you, but I didn't want to get to know you." I replied to him with the same response I gave Beryl, "Huh?"

His words caused me to do further self-evaluation of how I could leave people with such an impression. I realized that I was a man who longed for respect but held back from relationships. I was a man who willingly let others know the good qualities about me but hid feelings, and certainly hid anything that might be viewed as weak or fearful. I came to learn this way of living was a loss. A loss for me and for my friends. I didn't know it at the time, but I was a Shadow Lover: committed to self-protection.

The path to compassion and genuine relationships goes through the doorway of courageously admitting woundedness. With the right people at the right time we admit that we've been hurt by events, by other people's choices and by our own poor decisions. We admit that we are prone to believing the Enemy's lies about us—you'll never measure up, you're unforgivable, you're a failure and always will be. We admit that we try to cover up. We admit that we walk with a limp.

We may think that openness and vulnerability push people away, but these attributes move us toward others and draw them to us.

I mentioned above how one man said he didn't want to know me when we first met. A few years later I was a fairly different person. I was increasingly willing and able to let others see behind my public façade. His crucial influence moved me in a positive relational direction. During a follow-up conversation we had sometime later, I revealed to him the pain I was living in at the time, and the details of a sin I was hiding that I hadn't revealed to anyone.

He must have been shocked at my sudden forthrightness because after I told him the story, he asked, "Why have you told me this?" My response wasn't remotely professional, collegial, reserved, or hidden. It was from the heart and as honest an answer as I had ever trusted anyone with: "Because I hardly know you, and I couldn't care less what you think about me."

Bam! With that sentence I crossed a chasm of self-protection. I admitted weakness and sin. I let him see a flaw, a big one. Unintentionally, I revealed a truth about me: *If I know you well, I must keep certain things hidden from you because I can't afford to risk your response being less than respect and admiration for me.*

How ironic and how sad this is. The only ones with whom I could truly be myself were those I didn't know or whose opinion I didn't care about. With my best friends, or at least with those I felt I needed to impress, I wanted to stay on a certain impenetrable level. Just as I had at one time with Beryl.

Through that experience, and others like it, I learned I have wounds and vulnerabilities that can be entrusted to others. I learned that they do, too. I learned I walk with a limp, and so do they.

As I mentioned, one of the wounds I lived with for many years is the belief that my value is based on performance and other people's opinions of me. I'm still vulnerable to that one and need to consciously renounce it on a regular basis.

NOBLE LOVERS

When we love God and others with all our heart we become Noble Lovers.

These are men who courageously move toward others on a deeper level than the norm. They risk rejection by revealing themselves to others and willingly make the cares and needs of others a priority in their lives. It's easy to keep a distance from others—to stay safe, and it's easy to ignore the feelings and concerns of others—to stay numb. It takes effort to deepen friendships and to remain a faithful friend. Noble Lovers are willing to do that.

Was Jesus a man of compassion? Absolutely. He was the greatest lover of all in that he faced the agony of death to demonstrate his compassion. Here's a sampling of verses in the first two Gospels that refer to his compassion:

- "When he saw the crowds, he had compassion on them" (Matthew 9:36).
- "He had compassion on them and healed their sick" (Matthew 14:14).
- "I have compassion for these people" (Matthew 15:32).
- "Jesus had compassion on them and touched their eyes" (Matthew 20:34).
- "Filled with compassion, Jesus reached out his hand" (Mark 1:41 NIV '84).
- "He had compassion on them, because they were like sheep" (Mark 6:34).
- "I have compassion on these people; they…have nothing to eat" (Mark 8:2).

Jesus *was* a man of compassion. He felt joy, happiness, sadness, anger, loneliness, even agony as he went about life. Because he was aware of his feelings he was "moved with compassion" when he recognized similar feelings in others. This compassion allowed him to respond with comfort and concern to those who struggled.

How do we become Noble Lovers? *By coming face-to-face with our own pain, woundedness, and self-protective behavior.*

WHERE DO OUR WOUNDS COME FROM?

Many times our wounds are *self-inflicted*; they come from our own foolish choices. We pursue the escape mechanisms of alcohol, drugs, perfectionism, workaholism, or pornography. We stay safe by disconnecting from others and risk ending up living lonely, self-protective lives.

It's the kind of life that singers Simon and Garfunkel famously and ironically sang about: "I am a rock. I am an island. And a rock feels no pain; and an island never cries." It's the life too many men choose by staying safely at work or in their man caves at home.

Many times our wounds come from *others' selfish choices*. The more we trusted the people who hurt us, or the more authority they had, the deeper the wound they left. Just as God designed us with heart, soul, mind, and strength, we can be wounded in these same areas. For example:

- Heart wounds from close friends or family members result in *emotional* abuse.
- Mind wounds from a cruel teacher result in *intellectual* abuse.
- Strength wounds from a violent parent or coach result in *physical* abuse.
- And perhaps most destructively, soul wounds from a trusted pastor, priest, or mentor, result in *spiritual* abuse. When coupled with intimidation, physical or sexual assault, these result in the deepest of wounds.

For many men, our most significant wounds come from our fathers. This isn't always the case. Some men have been grievously wounded by their mothers or by other deeply trusted people.

Because their mothers were the ones who bore them for nine

months, gave birth to them, were connected to them by a cord, and nursed them on their breasts, children develop a profoundly deep bond—conscious and subconscious—with their mothers. Even if others don't understand them, or love them, Mom always will. Sadly, for some children, Mom didn't. She abandoned them, ignored them, or abused them. These are among the saddest stories we read or hear about. A Mother Wound, when it happens, is profound.

But for most men, it's their dads who pass on the deepest wound. The wound is so significant not only because of how Dad fell short, but because of what it causes us to believe about God. Children view God through the lens of their fathers. Kids think, "God is a lot like Dad, just way more so."

The truth is, fathers have not lived up to everything their children need. Why? Because their own fathers didn't, and they inherited the same wounded patterns their dads laid in their laps. For many men the most gaping holes in their hearts and souls are the wounds they got from Dad—the Father Wound. It's the difference between the father-longing God placed in the hearts of all children and the reality of what they got.

Because no father is perfect, and they all fall short in many ways, this father-gap is common: the dad with a short fuse, the dad whose self-image is too wrapped up in his work, or the father whose most emotionally honest moments are watching sports on TV.

For many men, this level of wound is fairly common. For others, however, the Father Wound is a Grand Canyon of unspeakable pain and rejection.

WHAT FATHERS ARE MEANT TO GIVE THEIR CHILDREN

What did God have in mind for fathers to give their children?

In Matthew 3:16–17 we see a snapshot of what God gave his Son. For 30 years Jesus had been virtually unheard of. And then, on the day described in this passage, Jesus was baptized. As he rose out of the water a "voice from heaven" spoke words of simple declaration and enormous power: "This is my Son. I love him. I'm proud of him."

We hear this statement again in Matthew17:5 on the Mount of Transfiguration when a few disciples saw a glimpse of Jesus' glory. The voice of God spoke and said those same three phrases with one profound addition: "Listen to him!"

Here's what boys need from their fathers in order to become healthy men. It's what God gave his Son:

Acceptance (we are wanted): Men need to know they are embraced and fully accepted by their dads. They need to hear their dads say, "That's my boy!" or "Hey, everyone, I'd like you to meet my son." Those words assure the son that he is seen, welcome, and wanted.

Affection (we are loved): "Man, I love him!" When a father says words like these in his son's presence, it demonstrates closeness, acceptance, connection, and safety with his dad. Some men pretend they don't need to hear those words; the truth is they long to know them. It proves to a son that the first man in his life loves him.

Affirmation (who we are): Men need to hear their dads say, "I am proud of you just the way you are." Sons need to know their dads are proud, not because of how well they reflect on their dads' image or uphold their dads' version of the perfect son. Sons need to know their dads are proud of *Who* they are, not just *What* they do or *How* they behave. Men need fathers who speak words that build confidence in their character, not just their behavior.

Anointing (who we can become): Men need to be seen, embraced, called out, and given a blessing by their fathers. They need to know their dads believe in them and see something about them that others ought to notice. Most moms are intuitive cheerleaders for their children; they instill belief in the value of who they are just because they belong to her. Dads are often blessers, that is, anointers. They instill in their children a belief in who they can become.

When Jesus heard the words of his Father at his baptism, he went from being an unknown son of a carpenter to the man who permanently changed history. Those words of *acceptance, affection,* and *affirmation* were later expanded to include *anointing* in the presence of Jesus' chosen disciples. When Jesus' Father said, "Listen to him!" in effect he was saying, "Pay attention. My Son brings something to the table."

When sons hear words like this from their dads, they receive a reservoir of significance and identity that can fuel a lifetime of impact. Men need acceptance, affection, affirmation, and anointing from their fathers. When they receive them, they are often launched on a path that changes the world around them.

What they often receive from their fathers is very different, though.

Too often the hearts of fathers have turned away from their children. As predicted in Malachi 4:6, destruction ensues and the consequences range from hurtful to dreadful. Because of their own woundedness—usually coming from their own fathers—all dads pass on some hurts and unhealthy expectations that harm their kids' sense of safety and esteem. In far too many families the damage is severe.

Their sons become men who experience wounds of:

Abandonment (physical distance): About 50 percent of first marriages in the United States end in divorce, and 75 percent of second marriages do. The consequence of these broken marriages is often physical distance between dads and their children. Of students in grades 1 through 12, 39% (17.7 million) live in homes absent their biological father (www.fathers.com). 92% of parents in prison are fathers (www.fatherhood.org).

What does that abandonment say to a boy? What did it say to you who have experienced it? Clearly, it says, "You're not wanted. You're not worth my presence." That's a wound that severely harms a boy's sense of worth.

Some of you men have gone through the agony of divorce. I can't imagine how painful that is. Regardless of the circumstances and causes, I urge you not to let a broken marriage separate you from your children. They need you. Of all the men in the world, only you are their biological father. You matter deeply to your kids, wherever they are.

Absence (physical presence, emotional absence): Some fathers remain present in the home but are sleepwalking through their roles. They spend too much time at work, the gym, the golf course, the sports bar, or in front of the TV. They may think they are fulfilling their role as a father just by being around, but in reality they may be doing more harm than good.

What does that emotional absence say to a boy? What did it say to you? "You're not worth my time or attention. I don't care about you."

Abuse (physical, intellectual, spiritual, or emotional damage): Some fathers unleash their own pain onto their kids. Not having dealt with their own anger, emptiness, or woundedness, they lash out at those closest to them. The film *Good Will Hunting*, for which Matt Damon received an Oscar for Best Original Screenplay, tells the story of a young man with a brilliant mind who kept it hidden because he lived a life filled with shame and self-condemnation. Eventually, through the efforts of a compassionate and persistent counselor, it comes out that Damon's character suffered horrific physical and emotional abuse from the hands and mouth of his violent father.

What does that kind of abuse say to a boy? What did it say to you? "You're bad. You're stupid. You're worthless. I hate you."

CONSEQUENCES OF THE FATHER WOUND

What are the consequences for those who have experienced abusive treatment from their dads? Scripture says the consequences of the sins of the father are passed on to their children for three and four generations (Exodus 20:5). The destructive inheritance a man receives becomes the damaged legacy he passes on.

Many of our families collect and pass on terribly broken stories—wounds—from one generation to the next. In the worst case, a boy grows up believing the message that he's not worth his father's presence, that he's not worth his father's time. Or that he's simply worthless. These are the deepest possible Father Wounds. At the very least the son grows up with a vague doubt as to whether he has what it takes to be a man.

All these messages from a father go directly to a boy's sense of worth and help shape his identity as a man.

Many men conclude that they need to work harder to please their fathers. Or they need to prove their fathers wrong. Or they need to measure up to what they suspect their fathers really wanted: a successful businessman, a star athlete, or a spiritual giant.

A friend of mine wisely observed, "The world rewards us for our wounds." If our wounds remain unacknowledged and unhealed, and if they take on manifestations of performance, competitiveness, and drivenness, there are numerous companies, teams, ministries, and churches that will gladly take advantage of those out-of-proportion compulsions. In the process, the wound not only remains unhealed; it gets infected.

My father was one of the finest men I—or most who met him—ever knew. Countless times through my childhood I was told what a wonderful man he was. And this was true. But even he gave me a wound: I never saw him sin; I didn't know if he was ever afraid; I never knew if he struggled with temptation, and I didn't know if he ever let others down or failed miserably.

I'm sure he experienced these things, but he never told me. A counselor friend eventually summarized it better than I could, "Craig, your dad loved you, but he didn't give you his heart." I was so accustomed to hearing my father only praised that my first recation to his accusation was denial. But as I let his words sink in, I realized he was on to something. My dad was a terrific presence and provider, but he did not trust me with the deepest parts of who he was.

Some of that was characteristic of his generation, some was his personality, some was his northern European cultural background, and some was *his* wound. Unfortunately, he laid some of that in my lap.

What it created in me was a commitment to be praiseworthy, to be admired, and to perform whenever asked to. Just like he did. Or to back away if I felt uncertain of my ability. And to cover up my own fears, struggles, temptations, and failures at all costs.

Because my dad was such an admirable man, I received one more wound—I didn't think I had the "right" to feel wounded. Craig, you should be grateful. Stop complaining, cover up, just *do* it. That is a wound that continues to heal, but I know I have passed some of this on to my own kids.

We see the resulting consequences of the Father Wound, in vary-ing degrees, in most of the men we meet. And they see them in us.

What do those scars look like? Men who are:

Angry: The Aggressive Man is committed to protecting himself by controlling others and circumstances. You scratch the surface of many men who are driven to success in business, in school, or on the sports field, and you'll find some anger.

Afraid: The Passive Man is committed to protecting himself by withdrawing to avoid yet another conflict or failure in his life. He avoids reminders that he may not really measure up as a man. You scratch the surface of men who remain on the sidelines of life—*and* most angry men—and you'll find fear. Fear of failure and fear of loss of respect.

Ashamed: The Searching Man is without direction or a sense of inner significance and value. He is at great risk of having his emotional foundation collapse if the "normal" worldly sources of self-esteem—performance, possessions, power, or prestige—are removed.

Not long ago I had coffee with a man who had at one time been a millionaire construction contractor, then lost his business and his home. He sat in a dark, somber mood and summarized his journey in two words, "I'm lost." Actually, he used three words, but one was an adjective I won't repeat here.

Men like him have no sense of identity apart from the praise of others or the rewards of the world. Perhaps they never saw or heard their fathers' pride in them simply for who they were, not just for what they accomplished or owned.

The Father Wound is the difference between what your heavenly Father gave you a deep longing for, and what you actually got from your earthly father. No human dad can fill that gap.

Sadly, this is yet another awful consequence of the Fall in the Gar-den, where at one time every heart-longing in humanity was satisfied through intimate relationship with a human partner and the heavenly Father.

And then it all fell apart. Because all humanity fell out of a perfect relationship with God, and because no human father is perfect, every son (and daughter) has this wound.

HOW DO WE HEAL THE FATHER WOUND?

The Father Wound is so deep that healing it is not a simple process. Most men carry a scar from this wound all their lives. The path to complete healing is a long one.

Acknowledge and grieve: The first step is to admit we have this wound, as well as others, that have seriously harmed us. We do, indeed, walk with a limp. We are no better or worse than those we see whose wounds may be more evident than ours.

Can you admit this? Can you admit that your choices, and the actions of others you trusted, have caused you pain and harm on a deep level? Can you admit that, while these wounds may remain hidden, at times they subtly yet persistently fuel some of your most hurtful behavior toward others?

Can you admit that the periodic explosions you unleash on unsuspecting family members, co-workers or inattentive drivers are the out-of-proportion responses to the anger, fear, and confusion residing just beneath the surface of your public persona?

I did.

I still do.

I think you can, too.

The first step toward genuine healing is to confess we have a problem. It's like acknowledging there was a fire in the foundation of our "home" a long time ago. That fire may have gone out, and the structure remains to this day, but the dead-giveaway smell of smoke still lingers on us, and others notice it even when we don't. Someday those charred joists in the foundation may collapse under the weight of the performance and protection superstructure we have built to cover them up.

Forgive: Secondly, we need to forgive those who have hurt or *are* hurting us. Our anger toward them does nothing to heal us; it only keeps us stuck in misery. They are wounded people, too. In his book, *The Bondage Breaker,* author Neal Anderson calls bitterness the "acid that eats its own container." We may think that when we stay angry with Dad or Mom or the boss or the wife, we are getting back at them. We may think we have them on the hook when in reality we are hanging ourselves on a hook. Everyone knows it but us.

Perhaps we live by the motto: "I'll show him. I'll be the pissed off son and I'll never let him forget it." Or, "I'll get back at her by making her miserable every time she's around our kids." That kind of resentful bitterness harms no one more than ourselves.

For our sake, and for the sake of those around us—the victims of our collateral damage who deserve none of this anger—we need to let this go. It takes a sincere plea to the Father, "Please, take this anger. I let it go. I don't want it any more. I leave revenge with you. I trust you to deal with it" (Romans 12:19).

Accept forgiveness: Third, we need to receive God's forgiveness for the choices we've made that have hurt us. We've all made poor choices and some of us have paid a steep price for those mistakes. I want to remind us of three passages.

As mentioned in chapter 2, Psalm 103:12 tells us how far our sin is from us when it says, "as far as the east is from the west, so far has he removed our transgressions from us."

Hebrews 8:12 confirms this when it says, "For I will forgive their wickedness and will remember their sins no more."

The third passage is from the book of Joel. The background is that the people of God have suffered one calamity after another. Their sin and unfaithfulness have brought wave upon wave of locusts to the point that the people have lost virtually all their food. Joel 2:12–13, 25 and 27 recount the message of the Lord:

"Yet even now," says the LORD, "return to me with all your heart, with fasting, with weeping, and with mourning; and rend your hearts and not your garments."

Return to the Lord, your GOD, for he is gracious and merciful, slow to anger, and abounding in steadfast love, and repents of evil.

"I will restore to you the years which the swarming locust has eaten…You shall eat in plenty and be satisfied, and praise the name of the Lord your God, who has dealt wondrously with you. And my people shall never again be put to shame."

"You shall know that I am in the midst of Israel, and that I, the Lord, am your God and there is none else. And my people shall never again be put to shame." (RSV)

Men, when we repent, that is, do an about-face from intentionally vengeful patterns such as anger, bitterness, and lack of forgiveness, God restores the years already eaten by locusts. He doesn't just forgive them, he repays them. And he ensures that we need not ever again wallow in self-condemnation and shame.

The miracle of God's grace is that he takes our wounds and our broken responses and he heals and redeems them. The scars may still be there, we may still walk with a noticeable limp, but he takes those wounds and softens our hearts with them. He makes us tender toward the pain of others, especially those in similar circumstances.

This is the source of compassion. It is the gift of redemption that God brings about through our wounds. He doesn't erase our scars as if they never existed. He allows them to remain visible and tender, but they now become a source of power, not woundedness.

Let me remind you of the primary points of 2 Corinthians 1:3–7:

- God is the Father of compassion and the God of all comfort.
- He comforts us in all our troubles, so we can comfort those in trouble with the same comfort we receive.
- Just as Christ's suffering flows into our lives, so does his comfort.
- That comfort brings about patient endurance for the suffering of others.
- Just as we share in suffering with others, we share in their comfort.

The man who loves God and others with all his heart has the compassion of a lover. He allows himself to be open with others and builds relationships of mutual trust and respect. This allows him to love others and others to love him.

With men he is not afraid to be courageous, sad, angry, or fearful. With women he demonstrates his ability to be trusted because he reveals his own vulnerability.

In short, he feels what others reveal; and reveals to others what he feels.

He lives out the words of Ephesians 4:31–32, "Get rid of all bitterness, rage and anger, brawling and slander, along with every form of malice. Be kind and compassionate to one another, forgiving each other [including those who have wounded us], just as in Christ God forgave you."

A godly man embodies the compassion of a lover. It's a powerful, manly, noble quality.

Who are the people in your life who need to see this quality in you?

QUESTIONS
FOR FURTHER THOUGHT OR DISCUSSION

1. How did your father express his feelings like sadness, fear, joy or anger? Did he show them in a way that caused others to feel safe, afraid or clueless?

2. How comfortable are you in showing emotions to others? If you're comfortable, where did you learn that? If not, do you have any idea why it's hard for you?

3. When it comes to compassion, which of these is most true of you: You were born compassionate; you are learning to be compassionate; you are becoming aware that you'd like to be more compassionate; you aren't compassionate at all?

4. A Noble Lover knows he's been wounded—he "walks with a limp." Have you been deeply wounded in any of these areas: Heart (emotions), soul (spirit), mind (intellect) and strength (physical)? If so, how has it made you tender or vulnerable?

5. How would you describe, in a few words, your mother's impact on you? Your father's impact on you? Did either leave a deeper wound than the other? What message did it speak to you: You don't matter; you're a disappointment; I'm ashamed of you. Put the message in your own words.

6. The steps to healing from any wounds, including those from parents, are: Acknowledge, grieve, forgive, accept forgiveness. Where are you on this journey of healing? What will it take to move to the next step?

CHAPTER 6

MENTOR: A MIND COMPELLED BY CONVICTION

We turn to the third image of what godly manhood looks like: *When we love God and others with all our mind, we have the conviction of a mentor.*

In her book, *Presence*, Harvard Business School professor, Amy Cuddy, makes the point that people make immediate gut-level evaluations of others based on two subconscious questions: "Can I respect this person?" and "Can I trust this person?"

I think this is certainly true for how most people evaluate professionals they choose, organizations they partner with, or individuals they trust. This is *always* how I have chosen car mechanics, doctors, handymen, financial advisers, and even dog breeders, to name a few. I subconsciously ask, "Is this person good at his job? Can I trust his character?"

Let's turn the questions around and ask them of ourselves:

Can people respect me? Am I good at "what I do," in terms of my work or the roles I fill in life? That question gets to the core of *competency*.

Can people trust me? That question gets to the core of my *character*. Character rests firmly on my *convictions*.

Later chapters in this book will get to our competency as men in the roles we fill in life. This chapter is about our convictions. A man who has rock-solid character is defined by a commitment to subject his decisions and actions to *internal convictions* rather than *external expectations or pressure.*

Convictions are all about what's inside my core. What resides at that level determines my attitudes and actions. One level deeper: our values determine our convictions.

Not long ago I heard the following quote (unfortunately, the speaker's name escapes me) at a Willow Creek Leadership Summit: "Don't just give people rules to follow. Give them values to believe in." That's extremely insightful. If, as parents, employers, or church leaders, we primarily focus on giving others rules to follow, they will only stand on a list of behaviors. As long as the list covers every possible behavior they will know what to think and how to act.

On the other hand, when we help instill deep, heartfelt values in our children, co-workers, or others we influence, they won't need to keep checking the rule list, nor will they need to keep coming to us for more rules. They will have a foundation of beliefs and convictions that govern how they live.

Second Corinthians 5:14 begins, "The love of Christ *compels* us…" (NKJV). The word "compel" is defined as "enthralling, captivating, inspiring conviction." I really like that language. Having grown up in a church that often focused on well-meaning obedience to rules, behavior, and external pressure, the word "compel" sounds joyfully liberating to me.

Rules and behavior are enforced from the outside and eventually become routinely dry. Compelling beliefs, and their resulting actions, come from an internal fire—a conviction—that is unquenchable.

Men of solid conviction have a clear sense of what is right and what is wrong. They can stand up and say firmly, "I disagree with that and won't do it," or, "This is what I believe in," when they are faced with temptation or see others behave in ways that break a moral code.

So, do our convictions matter? I'll answer firmly and unwaveringly:

It depends. It depends on what kind of men we want to be and what kind of world we want to live in.

Heroic Conviction

It helps to picture an actual event where people's convictions rose instinctively to the surface and affected others. You'll remember the incident in Tucson, AZ, when Rep. Gabby Giffords was shot in the head in a grocery store parking lot while conducting a voter drive. The men, women, and children who were all threatened by a sick person with a gun (need we point out, it was a man?) needed someone to forget about his own fear and confusion and step into danger. In other words, people urgently needed someone with conviction to come to their rescue.

Many unexpectedly did.

- Army Col. (Ret.) Bill Badger, 74, hit in the head with bullet fragments, was one of the first to grab the shooter.
- Patricia Maisch, 61, walked directly in front of the shooter and grabbed his extra magazine so he couldn't fire any more. When asked afterward how she could have done so, she replied, "You just do it."
- Joe Zamudio ran out of Walgreens when he heard the shots and launched himself onto the shooter, holding him to the ground until police arrived.
- Dr. Steve Rayle helped hold the shooter down, then went about tending to the injured.
- Daniel Hernandez, 20, Rep. Gifford's intern, held her in his lap, pressing his hand on top of her wound to stop the bleeding, probably saving her life.

These are genuine heroes. Only one of them was trained to face gunfire (and he never had before). None of them knew what to do once bullets started flying. They were stunned, shocked, confused, and afraid. Their physical and emotional experiences were the same as any of ours would be, but their responses and reactions stood out from the crowd. They instinctively took action on behalf of others. These were formerly anonymous people who reflexively chose to risk their lives for people most didn't even know. Deep, unseen, heart-level conviction burst to the surface and drove their behavior.

WHAT ARE WE PURSUING?

Let's return to our previous question: Do convictions matter? It depends on what kind of men we want to be and what kind of world we want to live in.

If what we want is to be men whose actions are largely self-centered, then, no, convictions don't matter. In fact, if self-gratification is our primary goal, whether conscious or not, then living a life of other-centered conviction hardly makes sense.

What are we pursuing in life? Is it:

• Prestige? Then we should commit ourselves to doing whatever it takes to impress others the most.

• Power? Then we should make decisions that control others.

• Possessions? Then we should take steps to acquire from others.

• Protection? Then we should behave so as to keep others at a distance.

• Pleasure? Then we should live a life primarily based on self-gratification.

You may see a pattern developing, other than the fact that these pursuits all start with P. The common thread is that these choices are self-directed. They all move in the direction of establishing self-satisfaction or self-protection as the ultimate priority.

As long as that is a man's priority, other-centered convictions don't matter. It takes no internal horsepower to make decisions and take actions that require no consideration of others. The man who lives solely for himself leaves a short-term legacy. Most of his impact ends when his life does. But what if we want our legacy to last beyond ourselves? What if we made choices where, rather than pursuing:

• Prestige, we stand up for others and make decisions that respect, honor, and defend others.

- Possessions, we give away and provide others the opportunity to have what they need.
- Pleasure, we seek genuine joy, which, because it isn't based on external circumstances, is deeper and longer lasting than mere happiness.

Ultimately the direction of each of these types of behavior is not self-centered. It is other-centered. As a result, it lasts longer.

The core conviction of immature, self-absorbed, not-yet-men is: My life is all about me. The core conviction of mature, genuine, noble men is: My life is all about others.

As young men grow into manhood, they are rarely exposed in their schools, colleges, or workplaces to a code of ethics or character that could be considered biblical. On the contrary, one of the highest values taught in many universities is the acceptance of virtually any belief as being legitimate. Truth is entirely relative and self-serving. The bottom line is: win. As a result, young men learn to present an image that is strong, tough, independent, and victorious, no matter the cost.

Sadly, the cost is a wavering, or non-existent, ethical standard that results in young men who are undependable, undisciplined, and destructive. According to 2011 (the last year that compared genders) FBI arrest statistics, males made up:

- 98% of those arrested for forcible rape
- 89% of those arrested for robbery
- 83% of those arrested for arson
- 81.7% of those arrested for vandalism
- 80% of those arrested for offenses against family and children
- 77.8% of those arrested for aggravated assault

SHADOW MENTORS

The presence or absence of a healthy father figure, or older male role model, has a profound impact on the next generation. Unfortunately, whether it's due to gang influence, a values-starved school district, exhausted parents, a lazy church, or a values vacuum at college, young men frequently learn a broken set of moral principles or simply establish their own system of right and wrong.

Men who waver in their ethics, who go with whatever is most popular or most convenient, are Shadow Mentors. Their ethical deficiencies can create ripples that affect the rest of their lives and the lives of others.

How badly corporations like Enron, Tyco, MCI, Adelphia, AIG, Lehman Brothers, and E. F. Hutton needed men (and women) to take a stand on their ethical beliefs a few years ago. Every one of these companies was at one time enormously successful in financial terms, but they were destroyed by men who lacked a strong moral foundation.

How awful to read reports of men like Representative Anthony Weiner, or Roger Ailes and Bill O'Reilly at the FOX network, Bill Cosby or Hollywood movie mogul Harvey Weinstein, who seemingly had a vacuum of conviction as they harassed, assaulted, or coerced women they had power over. Sadly, these men are not exceptions; they have just been brought out of the shadows. No doubt they were "mentored" by older men who convinced them their power came with the right to take advantage of others. They in turn indirectly mentor younger men who learn from their example.

Society is filled with men whose sole inner conviction appears to be: It's all about me. Men in the media and entertainment industry, such as those mentioned above, who will stop at nothing to get their way; men in business who swindle others out of millions to pad their own accounts; fraternity leaders who haze new recruits and pass on entitlement to unlimited party favors; prima donna athletes who strut and pose in the end zone as if they are the only reason they ended up there; media-driven evangelists who distort the Word and how God answers prayer in order to inflate their own wealth.

The list of Shadow Mentors is long. And it's nauseating.

NOBLE MENTORS

The epitome of men of godly conviction is the Noble Mentor. He is a man who has experience, knowledge, and wisdom—and who passes these on to others for their benefit. His primary concern is to respect, encourage, and lift up those he is instructing. He is passing on a legacy that will live beyond himself.

The Noble Mentor knows he is flawed. He has the wounds to prove it. But he has learned from his mistakes and is willing to reveal to others not just successes, but failures. He accepts his own limitations and looks for advice from others.

The Noble Mentor listens to older men who made wise choices and are now living truly joyful, successful lives. He also watches older men who have been down a path that led to destruction or emptiness. He not only takes these lessons for himself; he passes them on to others who can also benefit from hard-won wisdom. He focuses on what is beneficial and true about life and eliminates those thoughts, habits, and practices that either waste time or are of no benefit.

The Noble Mentor lives according to Philippians 4:8–9:

Finally, brothers, whatever is true, whatever is noble, whatever is right, whatever is pure, whatever is lovely, whatever is admirable—if anything is excellent or praiseworthy—think about such things. Whatever you have learned or received or heard from me, or seen in me—put it into practice. (NIV '84)

And 2 Timothy 2:2:

And the things you have heard me say in the presence of many witnesses entrust to reliable men who will also be qualified to teach others. (NIV '84)

Wow! Can we truthfully say, "Anything you have seen in me, pass on to others?" I'd have to honestly say "No," I wouldn't want to pass on to others "*anything* they have seen in me." But it is absolutely my hope that the older and wiser I become, the more others can benefit from watching and listening to me.

Pursue Wisdom

Noble Mentors are those who have their eyes on others. They actively seek out those who are younger or less mature—those who can benefit from their experience. Noble mentors are more concerned with passing on inspiration than information. They seek deep eternal truth that helps them live wisely and pass on a dynamic legacy.

How do we get wisdom? We ask for it. God longs to give his followers wisdom. But James 3:13–18 tells us there are two kinds of wisdom:

Knowledge that harbors pride, bitter envy, and selfish ambition. This results in disorder and strife. We see plenty of this kind of "wisdom" in the world.

Wisdom that comes from God. This is pure, peace-loving, considerate, impartial, sincere, resulting in righteousness.

Scripture is full of exhortations to pursue wisdom, but nowhere more directly than in Proverbs. Proverbs 2 urges us to: "…turn your ear to wisdom…call out for insight…search for it as for hidden treasure… the LORD gives wisdom…then you will understand what is right and just…wisdom will save you from the ways of wicked men…it will save you from the adulteress…thus you will walk in the ways of good."

And Proverbs 4:4–9 exhorts us to:
Take hold of my words with all your heart;
keep my commands, and you will live.
Get wisdom, get understanding;
do not forget my words or turn away from them.
Do not forsake wisdom, and she will protect you;
love her, and she will watch over you.
The beginning of wisdom is this: Get wisdom.
Though it cost all you have, get understanding.
Cherish her, and she will exalt you;
embrace her, and she will honor you.
She will give you a garland to grace your head
and present you with a glorious crown.

Men, do you see how deep and profound wisdom is? It determines the difference between self-absorbed, foolish lives and insightful, other-focused lives. Go after wisdom. Ask for it. Pray for it. God loves to grant it. But don't hold it to yourself. Pass it on to others. That's what a mentor does. He equips and empowers others.

SPEAKING TRUTH TO POWER

There is a term applied to those who stand up against organizations and individuals who wield unusual authority—even authority to harm those who criticize them. It's "speaking truth to power." Its first documented use was in a series of papers developed by the Quakers in the 1950s as they urged alternatives to violence in the conduct of the Cold War. The documents were called, *A Quaker Search for an Alternative to Violence.*

The first time I remember hearing the term was in reference to those who stood up to the shady power of the Nixon administration during the Watergate scandal. The phrase has come to symbolize the willingness of those in vulnerable positions to speak hard truth to those in powerful positions who might not want to hear it.

I once experienced a pattern of practices in a ministry that I thought was wrong. It wasn't sinful, but it bordered on being unethical or, at the very least, disrespectful of a certain group of people. I chose a different way of doing things, and I wasn't the only one. But we were a minority.

Over time it became clear that I was viewed with skepticism because of my views, and eventually I was told for the first time ever by a boss, "You aren't in the right fit." In effect, "Craig, you don't measure up."

As I look back I know that God redeemed that painful situation, and I'm glad I stood my ground. But I have one regret. I should have spoken truth to power more forcefully. I should have said to the person directly responsible for the decision affecting me, "This hasn't just happened to me. This is a pattern that has gone on for years, and everyone knows it. For the sake of this organization, please stop this pattern."

I wish I had said those words, but I didn't. As a result, I was not the last person to suffer the same consequences for the same reasons. If I could change things about that painful chapter of my life, it would be to speak truth to power for the sake of the organization and for the sake of those who remained after I left.

BIBLICAL MENTORS

Though the term "speaking truth to power" may be only 60 years old, the practice of speaking truth to power goes back quite a bit further:

Daniel, Shadrach, Meshach, and Abednego

The book of Daniel tells the story many of us learned in childhood of four young Israelites who defied the orders of King Nebuchadnezzar, their political authority, to bow before his idol and to cease praying to God. Even when Shadrach, Meshach, and Abednego were confronted with the threat of death they refused to obey.

They spoke truth to power.

Similarly, when Daniel was told to stop praying to his God, he didn't. In fact, he prayed three times a day in his room where the window faced Jerusalem. He engaged in an act of civil disobedience that Martin Luther King, Jr. would have been proud of.

Peter and John

After Jesus's home-going, Peter and John were told by the Sanhedrin, their spiritual authority, to no longer preach in his name. Acts 4 describes their encounter with power.

> Then [the Sanhedrin] called [the disciples] in again and commanded them not to speak or teach at all in the name of Jesus. But Peter and John replied, "Which is right in God's eyes: to listen to you, or to him? You be the judges! As for us, we cannot help speaking about what we have seen and heard" (vv. 18–20).

This was not the meek response the keepers of the Law were expecting.

Jesus

Countless times Jesus stood before the pious Pharisees, the stoners of women, the condemners of healing, the pompous legalists, the spiritual authorities of his day, and spoke words that silenced and condemned them. He got in their faces so frequently and so disturbingly that they eventually had him crucified.

I'm not recommending that we go toe-to-toe with our supervisors quite so confrontationally. I am saying we have the same authority on which to speak the truth. Daniel spoke truth to political power. Peter and John spoke truth to spiritual power. Jesus spoke truth to illegitimate power. So can we.

Perhaps more than any other character quality, speaking truth to power, standing up for our convictions, requires *heart.* The French word *coeur,* which is the root of our word "courage," means "heart." How do we demonstrate conviction? We live and speak with courage, from our hearts.

LIVING WITH HEART

I find acronyms are helpful for memory, and I've worked hard to squeeze the English language into something memorable and accurate in what follows, so please have patience with this. It's worth it.

How do we live with conviction and speak truth to power? By living and speaking from our HEART:

*H*onor our authorities and organizations: The book of Daniel tells how Nebuchadnezzar searched for the finest men to serve in his palace:

> The king talked with them, and he found none equal to Daniel, [Shadrach, Meshach, and Abednego]; so they entered the king's service. In every matter of wisdom and understanding about which the king questioned them, he found them ten times better than all the magicians and enchanters in his whole kingdom. (Daniel 1:19–20)

These four godly men were not troublemakers or passive-aggressive whiners. They stood head and shoulders above everyone else. Even though they had another God, they still honored Nebuchadnezzar's political authority over them.

Similarly, we should be men who honor those who are authorities, whether at city hall, at work, or at church.

Examine our motives and intentions:

> It's easy to see a smudge on your neighbor's face and be oblivious to the ugly sneer on your own. Do you have the nerve to say, "Let me wash your face for you," when your own face is distorted by contempt? It's this I-know-better-than-you mentality again, playing a holier-than-thou part instead of just living your own part. Wipe that ugly sneer off your own face and you might be fit to offer a washcloth to your neighbor. (Luke 6:41–42 The Message)

That's remarkably clear advice. Christians sometimes have a deserved reputation for demonstrating a holier-than-thou approach with others, whether neighbors, co-workers, or even Christians of other denominations whom we think will probably just barely make it into heaven.

This passage makes it unmistakably clear that before we go off on a rant about someone else's shortcomings we should take a good look in the mirror at our own practices and motives. Before standing on our convictions, we should take time to think this through, humbly examine our hearts and respectfully examine the other person's intent. We just might see another perspective.

Approach the right people: When we disagree with a new policy at work, or are legitimately concerned about a decision our pastors or elders have made at church, the easiest path is to find someone else just as aggrieved as we are and commiserate with each other. As they say, "Misery loves company."

This is neither a courageous nor an honest path. It's gossip. Simply looking for others to endorse our own point of view does little to bring about resolution or justice in a healthy way. We should approach the right people; those who actually made the decisions or policies we are struggling with, or who have the authority to make a change. We should not be passive aggressive, or brooding complainers behind our bosses' backs.

Represent: OK, here is where I shove a word into a predetermined box. This may not be the best word, but it's still the right step in this journey.

Represent. Speak up. Be honest. Speak for yourself and for others. Look at our previous biblical examples for this characteristic:

Daniel and his cohorts were blameless, model citizens and workers, until they were told to compromise a principle more important to them than their position or security. In the case of Shadrach, Meshach, and Abednego, they were told to bow down to an image. That's where they drew the line. Their message to authority was, "We will obey and honor you, but we will not worship you nor compromise our beliefs."

Daniel 3 describes what happened when they were brought before Nebuchadnezzar, who was "furious with rage." "How dare you disobey! I'll have you thrown into a blazing furnace! Then what God can save you from my hand?"

How did they respond? Represent. They respectfully, directly, courageously, and without apology stood for their convictions. Read Daniel 3:16–18. We know how the rest of the story went. They were spared. The king's soldiers who threw them into the furnace...not so much.

Daniel "represents" in a similar way with Nebuchadnezzar's son, Belshazzar, who saw some obscure writing on the wall but couldn't interpret it. Daniel pulled no punches when asked to translate the message. In essence he says, "O, Belshazzar, you have not humbled yourself, though you knew all this. Instead, you have set yourself up against the Lord of heaven...Your days are numbered, you have been measured and found wanting, your kingdom will be divided. That night he died" (Daniel 5:22–28, paraphrase).

As mentioned earlier, Peter and John's response to power as told in Acts 4 is essentially, "You do whatever you need to. As for us, we can't stop speaking about Jesus! And we won't." It's tough to stop that kind of conviction.

How about Jesus? How did he respond to threats and intimidation from authorities? He never backed down; rather, he spoke piercing truth. On what authority did Jesus speak so boldly? "I do nothing on my own authority," he said. "I have come with my Father's authority" (see John 5).

On what authority do we establish our convictions and speak up when we need to? The exact same authority. Others may not recognize God's authority, but that doesn't mean it doesn't exist.

"I am not here to please man!" Jesus said. Who are we trying to please when we confront dishonesty, injustice, and corruption? Do we let it slide or do we speak truth to power?

We represent. We represent our convictions; we represent on behalf of others; we represent the values and principles we believe God calls us to.

Take the Consequences: Just as in the above examples, we understand that speaking truth to power may well have some consequences for us.

Patrick Lencioni, well-known business author of *The Five Dysfunctions of a Team*, says that the best way to tell what your deepest values are is to note the convictions you're willing to get punished for. There will often be consequences when we take a stand. Sometimes positive consequences, sometimes very difficult ones.

Shadrach, Meshach, and Abednego survived a furnace and then were promoted by the king. Daniel survived the lion's den. The consequences for the men who accused him to the king were harsh; they were fed to the same lions, along with their wives and children.

God chose to honor Daniel and his fellow Israelites by having their authorities turn entirely to their position and then tell the rest of the world to do the same. It doesn't always work out that way, and it may not for you and me.

Peter and John stood up for their convictions. They were jailed and told to keep quiet, but were set free, "because all the people were praising God" for the miracle they had done. While John lived to an old age, Peter was eventually crucified, upside down at his request, for his beliefs.

Jesus was welcomed as a conquering king with palm fronds one day, and a week later was crucified for, among other things, speaking truth to power.

There are no guarantees what reaction those in power might have. Some might be persuaded, others might fight tooth and nail, still others might end their relationship with us. In all likelihood, none will kill or crucify us. In any case, the willingness to take the consequences of our convictions and actions is a crucial part of the equation when we talk about speaking truth to power.

Men of conviction do not rely solely on their own judgment because they know that it is flawed and can be tainted by their tendency to be self-centered. The Word of God is the tool that men of conviction use in their pursuit of truth.

They believe the truth of verses like Hebrews 4:12: "For the word of God is living and active. Sharper than any double-edged sword, it penetrates even to dividing soul and spirit, joints and marrow; it judges the thoughts and attitudes of the heart."

Men of conviction look to the guidance of God's Word to help them separate right from wrong. They use it as a sword that cuts error away from truth.

LOOK FOR A MENTOR; BE A MENTOR

During my first visit to the spectacular Glen Eyrie castle in Colorado Springs, CO, operated by the Navigators, I heard Larry Crabb give this description of a godly mentor:

> He is a man 15-to-30 years older than you who is walking down a path you want to walk. You respect the way he's walking that path, and you want to follow his example as best you can. You can see from his limp, and scars on his hands and knees, that he has had some stumbles; he doesn't hide them.

In fact, in the past he has even pointed them out to you when it seemed the time was right.

He walks ahead of you, every now and then turning to watch your journey. You can tell that while he has his own path to walk, he cares deeply about yours.

And then you stumble; you trip over a root in the path, or stumble into a pothole, and fall to your knees. You're embarrassed that you didn't see it. Your hands are scratched and your knees are scuffed.

When he sees you fall, the mentor does not impatiently turn away and leave you. He stops and watches. But he does not come to you to pick you up. With wisdom and patience, he waits and watches. He speaks encouragement to you, convincing you that not only does he believe in you, he is utterly convinced you now have the capacity to get up and move forward on your own.

You get to your feet, brush off your pants, regain your footing, and continue your journey. When you do, the mentor breaks out with a warm smile, turns, and keeps walking.

When I heard Crabb tell this story, my eyes welled up with tears. Why is that? It's because this story communicates something I long for, that I believe every man longs for. We want a wise older man to notice us, to allow us to follow him and learn from him. And when we stumble and make a mistake, he doesn't turn his back on us, nor does he pick us up; no, he stops and watches. Everything in his demeanor communicates, "I see you. I care about you. I believe in you more than you believe in yourself. And I'm not leaving."

Have you ever had a mentor like that? What would you give to have one? Perhaps there is a man who comes to mind right now. Why not ask him? Perhaps no one comes to mind right now. You may struggle to find one, but it's worth the effort, so keep looking.

Now consider mentoring from the other side of the equation; think about becoming a mentor to a younger man. Here's what I have found about mentoring relationships: Younger men long to have the attention of older men; just someone who will notice, pay attention, and care. Older men long to impact younger men's lives and to help them avoid some of the mistakes the older men have made.

Sadly, they can both disqualify themselves with wrong thinking: Younger men think, "I'm not worth noticing. I don't matter. No one cares what choices I make." Older men think, "What do I have to give? I don't know all the answers. I've screwed up enough for myself."

It turns out they are both mistaken. Younger men are not looking for perfection; they're looking for honesty. Older men are not looking for genius protégés, they just long to touch the future. They want to leave a legacy.

SAYING "YES!"

Men, what if we said, "Yes!" Yes to looking for and inviting an older man to speak into our lives. What if we overcame the hesitancy we might feel about taking the initiative and simply asked, "I notice you and think I can learn a lot from you. Would you be willing to be a mentor to me?"

For we who are older, what if we said, "Yes" to looking for a younger man whose life and circumstances matter to us. What if we overcame our hesitancy about taking the initiative to speak into his life and said, "I have my eye on you. Would you be willing to meet with me every now and then and let me speak to you about life lessons I've learned?" Most young men who have a thirst for wisdom would leap at that invitation.

I have personally benefitted from the mentoring of several men whom I watched and learned from simply because I respected the way they lived their lives and treated others.

My father, Neil Glass, a hospital administrator and ministry leader, demonstrated humility, gentleness, and kindness toward virtually every person he met. Though he had numerous responsibilities, he made a priority of family and any event that was important to my siblings and me.

Dr. Walt Liefeld, professor at Trinity Evangelical Divinity School and elder in the church I grew up in, was one of the first preachers I heard who spoke with such enthusiasm and conviction that it was as if he was talking directly to me. Years later, while offering some speaking advice to me, he said, "Craig, I always look for one person in the audience with whom to make repeated, lingering eye contact. When I do that it feels personal to the whole audience. By the way, when you're in the room, you're the person I focus on."

Dr. Earle Fries, director of the missionary training program Beryl and I went through at International Teams, got up early every Saturday specifically to spend a couple of hours studying the Bible. He loved the Word and loved applying it to everyday events we students saw in the headlines. Along with his wife, Julie, Earle also pastored Beryl and me and hundreds of missionaries overseas with warmth, kindness, honesty, and an ever-ready laugh.

Dr. Kevin Dyer, the founder and president of International Teams and Bright Hope International, encouraged Beryl and me to consider the value of nine months of training and a year smuggling Bibles. (We had a much shorter-term plan for missions in our lives.) As he did for literally thousands of people, Kevin saw potential in me that I didn't see. He elevated me to leadership roles that put me on the absolute edge of what I thought I was capable of. More than any other person in our lives, Kevin is the reason we remain in vocational ministry more than 40 years later.

When a man loves God and others with all his mind, he takes on the conviction of a mentor. He makes decisions based on principles and values, not just whatever others want him to do or whatever will get him ahead in the world. He accepts God's gracious forgiveness for the mistakes of the past, embraces a grace-filled calling, and puts others' well-being before his own. He is compelled by the conviction of a mentor.

Who are the people in your life who can benefit from the Noble Mentor in you?

QUESTIONS
FOR FURTHER THOUGHT OR DISCUSSION

1. What did your parents value most in life as you were growing up: Relationships, work, money, service to others, family, power, God, possessions)? Have you picked up some of the same values, or chosen completely different ones?

2. Who is a man you look up to as a role model? What do you admire about him?

3. Have you ever had a formal mentor? Have you ever mentored someone? How did those relationships happen? How did they go?

4. Read Galatians 5:22, 23. Which of these attributes come naturally to you? Which do you struggle with, or long for, the most?

KING: A SOUL ANCHORED IN CONFIDENCE

Have you ever met a bully? A boy who seemingly has no fear of others and lives each day with the thrill of intimidating everyone? Or a man whose force of personality and mere presence causes others to quiver? I'll bet you have. I've met several.

The first bully I ever met was in first grade. His name was Biff. I'm not kidding. In fact, when I saw the bully character Biff in the movie *Back to the Future*, I thought, "So that's where he ended up."

The Biff I knew struck terror in the hearts of all the other boys and girls. His whole demeanor—straight greasy hair, a sneer on his lips, pugnacious posture—was intimidating to say the least. He'd knock books out of your hands, pull girls' hair, and thought nothing of slugging any guy who crossed his path.

This was a six-year-old boy! Can you imagine what his family life or his fathering must have looked like?

One day, Biff and I had a standoff. I have absolutely no recollection of what it was about, nor if it was even worth fighting over. All I remember was the utter terror I felt, anticipating the pain he was about to unleash on my face. Thank goodness, before Biff could unload his barrage, a teacher separated us and walked us into the classroom.

Biff was the epitome of brute strength and frightful confidence. He strutted; others quaked. He showed up; others disappeared. Biff ruled the "mean streets" of Westbrook Elementary School.

FALSE CONFIDENCE

Do you have any stories like this? Encounters with a boy, a teen, a coach, a teacher, a supervisor, or a boss who brimmed with such confidence that he caused you to quake in sheer fright?

That's not the confidence I'm talking about in this chapter.

Some men have an air of intimidation about them that is tangible. They seem supremely confident. In control, sure of themselves, strutting with an air of arrogance, dominating conversations, never failing to give their opinion, always getting their way.

That's not the confidence I'm talking about. In fact, that behavior—rooted in dominance, posing, and intimidation—is not confidence at all. It's the exact opposite of the confidence God calls forth from a man.

The strut and posing of a bully is a mask intended to cover fear and insecurity through outward bravado and intimidation. You know what it looks like. It's frightening; it causes others to shrink back, to remain silent, to walk away, to allow the wearer to get his way.

But what lies just behind that aggressive mask is the bully's own world of fear. Whether he knows this or not, he is counting on others to shrink back so he won't have to reveal his own insecurity.

Perhaps you remember the "power ties" and tips on how to "dress for success" from the 1980s. There is something to be said for dressing appropriately for the setting, but relying on outward appearance, let alone a piece of fabric, for confidence is another form of wearing a mask. It's just a more presentable mask than bullying.

A man who hides a vacuum of self-worth can try to dress it up, or try to keep others at a distance, but sooner or later that real person inside is uncovered by his own actions and words toward others. Insecurity leaks.

Real confidence is much deeper than posture and clothing. It's a heart-level sense of assurance in your own value. Our parents—and especially for boys, our fathers—can build up our confidence by noticing us, spending time with us, lifting us up, and recognizing our worth and value. The importance of that solid foundation of significance communicated by the first man in our lives can hardly be overstated. Nor can its absence be easily compensated for.

Sadly, many men have had fathers, or mothers, who did not encourage them or lift them up; rather, they pulled them down either by criticizing and ridiculing them, or by ignoring them. These men often lack confidence, because deep inside they feel as if they do not have value. I bet anything Biff had a dad like that.

MASKS WE WEAR

In chapter 2 we talked briefly about masks we wear. Let's take it deeper. A man walking around with a lack of self-confidence can rely on many external props to try to fill the vacuum. We know these men. We might be one.

These props are the masks we learn to wear very early on in our lives; the ones that bring a measure of respect and admiration, but which we fear allowing to slip, lest others see what's beneath.

These masks look like:
- Accuser/Victim
- Stoic/Tough guy/Lone wolf
- People pleaser/Servant/Slave
- Performer/Impresser/Workaholic
- Perfectionist/Expert/Authority
- Intimidator/Attacker/Winner
- Legalist/Judge/Condemner
- Rebel/Anarchist
- Passive-ist (paralysis via analysis, or outright fear)
- Clown/Joker
- And more

While some of these masks are clearly unflattering, e.g., Condemner, others have an admirable aspect, e.g., Servant. When and where, let alone why, did we learn to wear these masks? The wearing of masks began long before we took our first breath. It started with the first man and woman.

"In the beginning," in the Garden, humankind was given everything we ever needed. God breathed life into our bodies and along with that life he breathed deep, profound longings. Everything people long for—safety, intimacy, significance, joy, peace, purpose, provision—was fulfilled through connection with God and his creation (Genesis 1:26–28).

And then, as we noted in Chapter 2, all this was all horrifically lost. When the first man and woman doubted God's goodness and suspected there was more to be experienced than what he had given them, their story, and the story of all their descendants, became a story of longing, loss, and covering up.

Take another look at Genesis 3:6–10. It relates the saddest story in the Old Testament. As soon as Adam and Eve acted on their distrust of God's nature, they experienced shame: "Then the eyes of both of them were opened, and they realized they were naked; so they sewed fig leaves together and made coverings for themselves" (v. 7). When exposed and totally known, their immediate reaction was to put on something to cover up.

God came looking for them, asking, "Where are you?" Adam's response reveals everything about the broken condition of his new relationship with God: "I heard you in the garden, and I was afraid because I was naked; so I hid."

I'm serious when I say that sentence makes me want to weep! The consequences are so global and personal at the same time! The confident condition of humanity's once joyfully fulfilled hearts and souls has utterly collapsed. When known and exposed, our new reaction is fear, shame, and hiddenness. As the Wycliffe Bible puts it, Adam said, "I hid me."

The first man and woman had everything and they gave it away. Their reaction was to find something that covered the nakedness; they thought they must cover who they truly were. We do the same.

In his book, *Inside Out,* Larry Crabb says, "All men and women are ruthlessly committed to self-protection." He's right. Once they gave away what they had, and discovered they were naked, the first man and woman became ruthlessly committed to self-protection. Even from God. You and I do the same. We just don't use fig leaves. We put on masks.

The list on page 123 shows only some of the ways we hide behind masks in order to keep safe or to impress. One problem with the masks we wear is that they all too often work for us. Performance gains respect. Workaholism gets promoted. Intimidation results in victory. The world rewards us for our wounds.

Yes, the masks actually do a very good job of getting us what we think we really want. And those who can benefit from our highly developed masks (be they ruthless businesses, dominant sports dynasties, violent gangs, or performance-driven churches) will happily reward us. As long as we keep it up.

We can even fool ourselves into thinking this routine is healthy. We convince ourselves we really *are* the mask. Call this the False Self. The mask becomes our source of pride, significance...and confidence.

But here's a sad truth about the masks we wear: Every one of them is a broken, limited response to the God-given longing we were built with. The Perfectionist is longing for acceptance; the Performer for admiration; the Passive Aggressor for safety and security; the Clown for joy. The Biffs in my life? They were truly insecure boys looking for respect. There's nothing wrong with longing for respect. They just took a violent path to find it.

TWO BROTHERS; TWO MASKS

In Luke 15, Jesus told a remarkable story about two brothers who wore completely different masks. The younger of the two, the one often referred to as the Prodigal Son, but whom I'll call the Rebellious Son, took everything his father had saved for him as an inheritance and squandered it. His mask was Rebel and he was looking for satisfaction of God-given longings—significance, joy, and freedom. His poor choices brought him to the depths of despair.

When he returned home, ashamed, convinced he no longer deserved to be called son, his father embraced and welcomed him. The father Jesus described did not cast shame or condemnation on the Rebel; he gave him what he was actually longing for—significance, joy, and freedom.

The elder brother, whom I'll call the Resentful Son, exposed his Performer mask when the father welcomed home the Rebel. The resentful son blurts out, "I've never left home! I've done all the work around here! You've never celebrated me!" He's longing for love, respect, and acceptance.

Had we been this guy's father, we might have been tempted to respond with the back of our hand. Not this father. He reveals God's heart when he says, "Son, you've always had my love. Everything I have is already yours. Come on, let's celebrate." He offered this son what he was actually looking for—love, respect, and acceptance. Intriguingly, Jesus' story ends without revealing whether the elder son forgave his brother and accepted his father's invitation to celebrate with them. We can see him going either way, can't we?

We all follow the pattern of these two sons. We take on the mask that we think is going to get us what we want. The deceit of the world is that it often does…for a while; until the mask slips, or the world moves on to a man with a better mask. Ultimately masks won't get us what we crave. Instead, they deplete us. People-pleasing, a longing for acceptance, leads to exhaustion; Piety, a longing for admiration, leads to legalism; being the Loner, who longs for safety, leads to, well, loneliness.

A LITERAL HORROR STORY

This pattern was clearly predicted in the Old Testament. I refered to this passage in Chapter 3, but I must turn to it again. Jeremiah 2:12–13 describes the core of our problems in finding genuine confidence:

"Be appalled at this, you heavens,
and shudder with great horror,"
declares the LORD.

"My people have committed two sins:
They have forsaken me,
 the spring of living water,
and have dug their own cisterns,
broken cisterns that cannot hold water."

As the above words say, this literally IS a horror story. We are making two tragic mistakes:

1. In our desperate pursuit to quench our thirst for the God-given longings we desire, we turn our backs on him—the One who actually IS the source of living water!

2. We make matters worse by frantically digging our own "cisterns," which fail us because they can't hold what we need.

We hope performance and success will satisfy our longing for significance and confidence. They don't, because they can't. They are broken cisterns incapable of holding the water we are looking for.

Our longings are God-designed; our self-serving pursuits for relief are ineffective. There is one source that quenches our thirst for all that we long for: God, "the spring of living water."

When God revealed himself to humanity in Jesus, he reminded us again: "...Let anyone who is thirsty come to me and drink. Whoever believes in me, as Scripture has said, rivers of living water will flow from within them" (John 7:37–38).

That "living water" is the only source that truly quenches our thirst for: significance, security, love, respect, intimacy, and joy. When the God-given longings we all have are satisfied by God himself, we are filled to overflowing with genuine confidence.

REAL CONFIDENCE

A man of real confidence knows his significance is ancored in two truths: 1. What God thinks of him, and 2. What Jesus did for him.

Psalm 139 is a chapter fully dedicated to describing God's magnificence. He is all-knowing (vv. 1–6), ever-present (vv. 7–12), all-powerful Creator (vv. 13–16), and wise judge (vv. 17–24).

In illustrating God's power in verses 13–16, the author, David, tells the story of your design in very specific, personal language:

- God created your inmost being
- He knit you together in your mother's womb
- You are fearfully and wonderfully made
- Your design was not hidden from God; he made you in the secret place
- You were woven together in the depths of the earth
- God saw your unformed body
- God knew every day of your life before even one of them came to be

Men, I don't know how you react to these words, but I want you to receive them personally. This is very specific language. God knew you, created you, watched you, and wanted you!

Do you believe all Scripture is God-inspired? That David wrote these words under the guidance of the Spirit? If your answer is "No," then I'm not sure how you pick and choose which passages to trust in and which to disbelieve.

On the other hand, if you do believe that Scripture, including this passage, is God's way of telling us truth about himself and about how he feels about us, this makes ALL the difference. It lays a foundation of significance and genuine confidence, which the broken cisterns of the world can never duplicate!

A man of rock-solid confidence knows how God feels about him. Alimighty God, the one true God of the universe, created him on purpose. That's confidence.

CORE TRUTH

A man of confidence also knows what Jesus did for him. Jesus died for him.

Romans 5:8 puts it as succinctly as possible: "But God demonstrates his own love for us in this: While we were still sinners, Christ died for us." Even while our ancestors had turned their backs on God, Jesus became human specifically to die in their place. He did that for you, too.

Here, I want to take a moment to divert toward this larger, crucially important topic. If you have never thought through the significance of the life and death of Jesus, this is, without question, the most important subject for you to explore. Nothing else comes remotely close.

Perhaps you've heard or read the verse that says, "This is how much God loved the world: He gave his Son, his one and only Son. And this is why: so that no one need be destroyed; by believing in him, anyone can have a whole and lasting life" (John 3:16 *The Message*). The whole point of Jesus's life was to die in order to bring you eternal life.

Jesus himself said, "I am the way and the truth and the life. No one comes to the Father except through me" (John 14:6). If these words are true, this changes everything. Your hope for spiritual fulfillment, joy, and salvation is based uniquely in who Jesus is and what he did for you. I urge you to consider taking him at his word and basing your spiritual hope on him.

So I'll say it again, a man of rock-solid confidence knows how God feels about him. God created him on purpose. He also knows what Jesus did for him. Jesus died for him. These truths provide unshakable confidence.

A man of real confidence knows he has flaws and weaknesses, but those don't undermine his sense of who he is. Those shortcomings don't determine his value; nor do they determine ours. God does.

I want you to let that sink in. A real man has nothing to hide, nothing to prove, no one to bully. That's a confident man. Our confidence is not based on the world's acclaim. It is based on the character of God and how he views us: unique, beloved, forgiven, and celebrated.

SHADOW KINGS

Mark 12:30 tells us to love the Lord our God with all our soul. When we do that, we have the Confidence of a King. We reflect the kingly authority of God to others around us.

Throughout history, kings have borne the image of power and authority perhaps more than any other kind of ruler. The king had ultimate control over those he ruled. His authority was unquestioned because he usually had very powerful resources at his fingertips.

However, kings demonstrated enormous differences in how they used their power. Think of King Herod, who was so threatened by rumors of Jesus' birth that he had all male babies of a certain age in Bethlehem slaughtered. He was a powerful man, but not a confident man. He was a bully of enormous proportions.

Herod is an example of the Shadow King or the Wounded King. He is a person in power who is convinced his significance and his own status, wealth, and authority determine his worth. History has been filled with such Shadow Kings. These are men (though there have been some women, too) who control and intimidate others. They accrue wealth, mostly by stealing it from others, and attack anyone who gets in their way.

Attila the Hun, Vlad the Impaler, Adolf Hitler, Joseph Stalin, Pol Pot, Idi Amin, and Saddam Hussein are just a few of the more egregious "political kings" who ruthlessly used their authority for personal glory and the destruction of those who opposed them. The use of their power was for self: self-protection, self-promotion, self-advancement, and self-aggrandizement.

This same pattern is also seen in some wounded "business kings" who have had the same commitment to self-promotion and the oppression of others: their numbers include business tycoons of the 19th century who attained enormous wealth by gobbling up land or others' businesses; the gangsters of 1920s Chicago; inner-city or suburban gang leaders who rob, kill, and destroy to protect their tribe and turf.

Then there are the modern-day moguls and "banking kings" who recently led the world into the greatest economic collapse since the Great Depression, and profited from it. These are wounded Shadow Kings.

Let's bring this closer to home. You may not see yourself as a "king" of any sort, whether in business, politics, or in neighborhood turf battles. But every one of us has realms of authority in life. If you are a middle school teacher, president of your homeowners association, husband and father, night-shift manager at a warehouse, coach of your daughter's softball team, Bible study leader, team lead at a fast food restaurant, you are a "king" in that realm. This role comes with a degree of responsibility and authority. You can use your position for the benefit of others or to promote your own self-serving agendas.

When Beryl and I moved into a new neighborhood several years ago I served for a term as the president of our homeowners association (HOA). The role mostly involved mediation concerning everything from fencing disputes to bargaining over house color and landscape design to granting exceptions for RV parking and raising rabbits. Not exactly the community-building experience I was anticipating.

As we built our team, a man I'll call Vic kept volunteering for sergeant at arms, or community patrol officer, anything that involved a level of authority and a slightly militaristic title. Not only did we not really have those roles, but I quickly saw that Vic had a quick temper and strong opinions of how "his" neighborhood ought to function. I also knew Vic had a handgun conceal-carry permit.

When my term was up, Vic threw his hat in the ring for the job. I didn't think he was the best candidate to wield that degree of authority, and neither did the HOA board. They chose a more qualified candidate as our next "king."

A Shadow King, regardless of the scope of his "realm," pursues positional authority. He takes advantage of title, position, and power to coerce and control others. He doesn't trust or empower others. He looks out for himself. The motto emblazoned on his royal crest is: "It's all about me." This style of self-serving leadership produces fear, insecurity, resistance, and distrust in followers.

NOBLE KINGS

Shadow Kings use power and authority primarily to advance their own agendas and expand their territory. Noble Kings work for the benefit of the community.

We read of biblical kings like David who, although he demonstrated shocking self-centeredness, e.g., having one of his warriors killed in battle so he could take the man's widow, was nonetheless described as a man after God's own heart (Acts 13:22). Sinful? Yes.

Imperfect? Without question. But David was also filled with the assurance that God loved him, forgave him, and granted him favor.

Similarly, the world has been blessed with noble political leaders who have served with character for the benefit of their followers. Men like Henry IV of France, George Washington, Abraham Lincoln, Winston Churchill, Mahatma Ghandi, Martin Luther King, Jr., and Nelson Mandela.

What does a Noble King look like? He is less concerned with pursuing *positional* authority than in demonstrating *moral* authority. He has shown a willingness to follow others respectfully. He knows he's flawed and won't hesitate to admit those flaws to the right people at the right time. He surrounds himself with others he trusts who use their own giftedness in order to compensate for his weaknesses and compliment his strengths.

He honors God as his ultimate authority. He uses his talents, roles, and opportunities to take action and make decisions that elevate and benefit others. He is committed to serving others, not himself. The motto on his crest is: "A life of service."

James 4:6 says, "God opposes the proud, but shows favor to the humble." If we use our strength in a humble way, realizing it comes from God and not from us, he will lift us up and use us to help others.

This style of noble leadership produces honor, respect, security, and submission in followers. They are willing to submit to this kind of leader because they know he has their best interests at heart.

JESUS AS KING

When we envision leaders of unquestioned earthly power and authority, Jesus is the antithesis of that kind of king. He was rejected by his own people; he was a man of sorrows, well acquainted with grief (Isaiah 53:3), from his lowly birth to the indescribable torture and agony of his death.

But when Jesus encountered pious religious promoters of the law, he stood face-to-face with them and spoke of his authority. His was not a worldly authority; he calmly confronted them with a power granted by God (John 7:28; 10:18; 14:10). I love how Jesus confidently, boldly rebuked those with earthly authority and clearly claimed a much higher authority.

Not only did he rebuke religious authorities, Jesus rebuked political authorities who threatened him with their power over life and death. He was not intimidated by Pilate: "You would have no authority over me if it were not given to you from above" (see John 18 and 19). Hmmm, good point.

Jesus also rebuked the spiritual authority of Satan, "the god of this world," when he was tempted in the wilderness (see Matthew 4).

Here is a confident man, fully aware of his own significance based on who his Father is. We can demonstrate the very same confidence. Jesus was "the Son of God," and if we have embraced him as the Lord of our life, so are we.

"You are all sons of God through faith in Christ Jesus…God sent his Son…that we might receive the full right of sons. Because you are sons, God sent the Spirit of his Son into our hearts, the Spirit who calls out '*Abba*, Father.' So you are no longer a slave, but a son; and since you are a son, God has made you also an heir" (Galatians 3:26; 4:4–7 NIV '84).

This means we can rest in the knowledge that we are loved and accepted for *who we are,* not *for what we do.*

This is the foundation of the confidence of a godly man: that the One who created us says that we have worth for all eternity. Our earthly fathers may have failed us, but the heavenly Father has lifted us up to a place of great honor in his eyes. We are no longer slaves; rather, we are sons, heirs to the King of Kings and Lord of Lords.

Truly confident men have a deep internal sense that they are valued. They know what results in genuine confidence—relying on God—and what results in false confidence—relying on posturing and masks.

Truly confident men, in turn, can pass blessing on to others through their actions and words. Through God's design, their words echo the voice of God to those they address. Confident men don't think they are better than other people, nor do they believe that they are less than others. They have a solid assurance that forms the bedrock of their lives.

In order to be this kind of man we need to claim our birthright. We need to remember who our Father is. And we need to remember who we are: his heirs. In embracing that role we can humbly and firmly live with the Confidence of a King.

Jesus said, "Love the Lord with all your heart and with all your soul and with all your mind and with all your strength....Love your neighbor as yourself" (Mark 12:30–31). When we follow that calling as a man, we live as:

Lover, with a Heart moved by Compassion

King, with a Soul anchored in Confidence

Mentor, with a Mind compelled by Conviction

Warrior, with Strength motivated by Courage

In our own efforts to live out these roles we will fail. Or at the very least we will fall miserably short, as we so often have in the past. But I'm convinced that when God made us as men, he made us capable of these qualities. In fact, they are in us already. They have been wounded, they have been suppressed by shame and they have laid dormant over the years. But every now and then they rise to the surface. That's because they reside in us. That's because we're men.

Women have their own God-given and God-revealing, magnificent qualities. I deeply celebrate that truth. But this is a book written to men, and so it's to you men I am speaking. When we remove the masks of the false self—the shadow—and allow God to reveal our true noble identity, he will bring out these manly, Christ-like qualities in us.

QUESTIONS
FOR FURTHER THOUGHT OR DISCUSSION

1. What, if any, messages did you hear from your parents or other authority figures that caused you to question your confidence, value or significance?

2. On what are you most tempted to base your sense of personal value or significance: Possessions, power, prestige, performance? How can you overcome this tendency?

3. Read Psalm 139:13-16 and Romans 8:14-17. What do these passages demonstrate about your value in God's eyes?

4. Has anyone in your life spoken blessing or anointing over you? When? Where? Why? What did that feel like?

5. What roles of authority do you currently have in life: Father, grandfather, uncle, supervisor, pastor, team leader? Have you spoken, or could you realistically speak, a King-like blessing to someone in your life? To whom?

PART III
LEGACY

CHAPTER 8

LEAVING A
LIFE-GIVING LEGACY

"Get rid of your junk or move!" Those unsettling words were spoken years ago when a village near Chicago took action against one of its families. For generations the family had been living in a rural area on the outskirts of the city. It had now become engulfed by relentlessly expanding suburbs. The family had a business at their home—collecting, storing, and selling junk.

This was more than just an odd lawnmower by the side of the house or a used car parked in the driveway. It was piles of rusting debris: tractors, washing machines, a forties-era Greyhound bus, and the fuselage of a DC3 airplane. Let's face it, if someone has a DC3 in their backyard, sooner or later it's going to start annoying the neighbors.

Eventually the village gave the family a choice; either get rid of all of their junk or move. The local newspaper interviewed the head of the household, asking him what he thought of the ultimatum. "It's unfair!" he responded. "Our family has been collecting junk for years. That's all we know how to do."

A lot of our families are like that. We collect junk. We collect wounded relational habits, dysfunctional communication patterns or sinful lifestyles. They become an accepted way of living that may, in fact, seem normal to us.

Not only do we collect them, we pass them on. Intentionally or not, they become our legacy to others.

Proverbs 13:22 touches on this concept. In *The Message* it says, "A good life gets passed on to the grandchildren." A godly man leaves a legacy for the next generations, for those who live beyond him, not just his children but those whose lives he touches every day—family, friends, neighbors, and co-workers. They are the ones to whom a legacy is passed. A godly man leaves a good one. An unintentional man passes on junk.

Several years ago I had a transforming realization. I worked for an organization that trained and sent missionaries throughout the world. One of my responsibilities was determining who was prepared for the demands of cross-cultural ministry and who was not.

Working with these candidates, I started to see a recurring pattern. For those who were clearly hindered by relational or emotional issues, the root of the matter almost always went back to their relationship with their fathers. They had "father wounds" that were not healed. This affected their view of themselves and their view of God, and they were still living with visible scars.

The lesson is inescapable. Men influence lives; we affect others for better or worse. That's why it is so important that we consider both the inheritance we received as well as the legacy we want to pass on. Our inheritance is poured into us; our legacy pours out from us. God calls on us to closely examine our inheritance and open ourselves to his transforming work so that our legacy is a blessing instead of the continuation of a curse.

We are all creating our own legacies. The key question is: What kind of legacy will it be?

WE RECEIVE AN INHERITANCE

Our inheritance is more than just a financial endowment. It's all the factors that make us who we are today. It's what we receive from our "soil," most significantly our parents, our culture, our schools, and our places of worship.

Part of our inheritance is the assumption that our way of doing life is mostly correct, and others' ways are varying degrees of wrong. Our parents may reinforce this through comments such as, "I don't care how others do it; *our* family does it this way." Certainly our churches place a strong emphasis on the rightness of their faith and practice. Other faiths or denominations are a little bit—or a lot—off.

This self-centered approach toward life and the convictions on which it is founded can become part of the junk we collect and pass on. Unless we open ourselves to the healing nature of transformation we will pass on those same wounded convictions to others.

We had no say in determining our inheritance, but our legacy is ours to create. Our legacy moves outward from us. It is the impact and influence we pass on to others. Legacy is that part of us that lives in other people and continues in them after we're gone.

A few years ago I shared a truly powerful experience with my father. He grew up in a Christian family in an Irish neighborhood on Chicago's south side. One day he called and said, "I'm going down to my old neighborhood today to visit my parents' gravesite. Do you want to come along?" Though I was in my forties, I had never seen his childhood home or the gravesite of my grandparents. I jumped at the opportunity and said, "I'd love to!"

Driving down the expressway to the south side, I expected some new insights into that neighborhood. What I didn't anticipate was that we would be visiting my father's inheritance.

Finding the street where he grew up, we parked and looked at the houses. Dad pointed out his house and where he and his pals played softball and football in the street. He told me the names of all the families that lived there: the Sullivans, the Kellys, the Burkes, and the McCredies. They were Irish immigrant families whose fathers worked as firemen, policemen, or street workers.

By this time I was starting to get a different mental picture of my dad. I didn't see a man with white hair and wrinkles whose stride was shortened by arthritis, but a young, active boy with red hair and freckles, full of energy, playing 16-inch softball.

We drove to his high school, Calumet High. Classes were not in session that day, but the doors were open, so we walked down the halls and into the cafeteria. He pointed and said, "Over there in that corner, that's where I always ate lunch." I saw a red-haired teen eating a peanut butter sandwich, six decades ago.

In the P.E. wing we walked through a hallway with a collection of old photographs, one of which was the 1940 football team. There he was, the center, holding the football. He knew every name of those pictured—characters from a season played long ago.

I realized I had embarked on a trip into the past with my father; that he had a long and deep story, a story that was the preface of my own.

The most powerful part of that day occurred at the cemetery where his dad and mom were buried. We found our way to the gravesites and stood in silence beneath the leafy canopy of a majestic oak tree pondering those two lives that had made such a profound impact on my father's own: Neal Morgan Glass and Katherine McLean Glass.

Finally, Dad asked, "Do you mind if I pray?" He prayed a relatively short prayer, but he ended with four words that have stood out to me ever since. He thanked the Lord for his family and for his father, and then he said, "I have no regrets." A man, almost eighty years old, who can say he has no regrets. Remarkable.

I thought, *What a father my grandfather must have been.* I was moved to be closer to him somehow, so I knelt next to Grandpa's gravestone. I just wanted to be in some kind of contact with this man who was a part of my story so long ago. He died when I was two or three years old; I only remember faint images of sitting on his bed just prior to his death. He called me, "My wee li'l man." I placed my hands on his headstone and traced the letters of his name with my fingers. Neal Morgan Glass. *Grandpa, thank you so much for being the kind of dad you were.*

He was born in a dirt-floor cottage in Northern Ireland, moved to Chicago as a young man and spent his adult life as a streetcar motorman, driving the significant and the insignificant alike through the busy streets of the bustling city. He was not a wealthy man, not an important man in the world's eyes. Few would call his a "success story." Yet he provided for and raised a family, he was faithful to his wife and children; he was a godly man and he passed on a rich spiritual legacy to my father.

I realized Dad might want to be alone so I went to the car and watched. To this day I can still picture him standing silently by his parents' gravestones beneath that huge oak tree on a perfect summer day. The sun shining through the branches, etching shadows on the lawn, a cool breeze rustling the leaves.

When he returned to the car, I said, "Dad, I want to let you know something." I hardly even knew how to say what was on my heart. "I realized just now that someday, that will be me standing under that oak tree, and I'll be looking at your headstone. I don't know if you'll be able to see me, and I doubt you'll know what I'm thinking, but I want to tell you right now what will be on my mind. I'll be thanking God for you. I'll be thanking God for the kind of man and the kind of father you were. And I'll have four words on my mind: *I have no regrets.*"

Have I led a perfect life? Absolutely not. I've had disappointments and I've stumbled in a number of ways. Did I have perfect parents? No—great parents, but certainly not perfect. But I had a father who was faithful, who was present, who was loving, who received an unusual inheritance from his father, and who passed on a wonderful legacy.

Both of my parents are gone now but my dad passed on the legacy he received from his own father of qualities that are becoming increasingly rare in our society: dependability, faith, self-sacrifice, and humility. He embraced these qualities and allowed them to define his life. The inheritance he received became his own legacy. Thanks to the choices of my grandfather and my father, I can look at what God has brought into my path and truly say:

LORD, you alone are my portion and my cup;
you make my lot secure.
The boundary lines have fallen for me in pleasant places;
surely I have a delightful inheritance. (Psalm 16:5–6)

WE PASS ON A LEGACY

Inheritance is poured into us; legacy pours out from us.

All of us have two primary needs: the need for *intimacy*—safe, genuine relationships with other people—and the need to make an *impact*—to know that our existence matters. (I am indebted to Larry Crabb for his insights about human needs on the deepest levels, especially in his book *The Marriage Builder*.)

There is a deep desire in our hearts that compels us to influence the world and the lives around us. It is that same desire that inspires us to consider the legacy we will leave behind.

Jeremiah 32:18 is both powerful and disturbing. "You show love to thousands but bring the punishment for the fathers' sins into the laps of their children after them" (NIV '84). These words are enormously convicting. When we sin, when we're proud, when we're short-tempered, when we're selfish, our sin doesn't only affect us. We fathers pass on our patterns of sin. They are laid into the laps of our children and our children carry them.

One of the pieces of junk my family collected was the belief that others' opinions of us determined our value. I allowed myself to believe my worth was primarily based on the impression I made on others, and that it had better be good. It's not that my parents, teachers, or church leaders specifically said so, but I picked up subtle clues and came to my own conclusion that my value was based on performance. That became an underlying assumption upon which I based my life. Sadly, that message didn't remain just with me; it became a piece of junk I passed on to my kids.

My daughter, Barclay, is a wonderful woman, but when she was a little girl, she was a blonde bombshell of determined energy. She was affectionately known at Sunday school as the "White Tornado." One evening, the board chairman of the ministry I worked with came for dinner. The house looked wonderful, the kids were behaving. Every family member was doing a great job making a good impression on this important man.

After dinner the kids went upstairs while I carried on a conversation with my friend. Soon the kids starting to race around, playfully yelling at each other. So I said, with infinite patience, "Excuse me, Bob. Hey, kids, calm down up there. You need to be quiet."

About thirty seconds of quiet passed and then the yelling began again. A second time I interrupted our conversation and called up to the kids, with a bit more intensity this time. "Kids! Dad said to be quiet, so please obey." This only produced about twenty more seconds of silence before the yelling started again.

Finally I realized there was no more hiding it—Bob now knew the truth about me. I was not able to control my own children. "Excuse me, Bob," I said with a forced smile and superficial chuckle, "I've got to take care of something here."

I went upstairs appearing calm and collected, but as soon as I got to the top of the stairs I saw Barclay running out of my son's bedroom screaming. Something snapped. I grabbed her, lifting her off the ground, went into my bedroom, and threw her on the bed. I looked directly into her eyes, hovering inches over her face, and with all the rage behind my embarrassment I hissed at her, "You keep quiet! Don't you *ever* disobey me when we have company!"

I never came so close to striking one of my kids in anger as I did that night. This was my daughter, whom I love, yet I exploded at her. I left her lying on the bed—terrified—and returned to a polite conversation with Bob over my wife's outstanding carrot cake a la mode. Barclay kept quiet.

Something was profoundly injured in my daughter that night. I demonstrated to her that Daddy is not always safe. To this day, every time I'm reminded of my behavior my eyes fill with emotion.

Later that evening as I thought through my reaction, I asked myself, *What was that all about? That was a piece of junk, Craig. You just proved your conviction that you must impress others at all costs. Nobody, not even your daughter, is going to expose you as being less than competent.*

I might as well have looked my daughter in the face and said, "Don't you dare show anybody that we're not a perfect family. Don't reveal the truth about us." I needed this man to think well of me, even at the risk of my own daughter's spirit. What a tragedy!

Later I apologized and let her know I had acted wrongly. Of course, she immediately forgave me, as little girls do. But the damage was already done. I had unwittingly exposed a deeply held belief—I must appear competent—that, in fact, was a wound. That wound had never been healed. As a result it became part of the legacy I passed on to Barclay.

She also struggles with the same over-concern with the opinions of others. In a recent conversation, she described past and current relationships where she spent a lot of time making sure friends were happy. "I was hurt by them a lot and often very afraid of making them upset," she admitted. "It became more about what they thought of me than having a true friendship."

Fortunately she sees herself making progress in this area through the support of her wonderful husband and a deeper understanding of how God actually views her: He loves her unconditionally just as she is. She also let me know, "You've come a long way too, Dad." Whew!

The good news is that God can transform us through his Holy Spirit. Christ-followers are no longer just natural descendants. We are now children of God. Yes, our sins are laid in the laps of our children, but we are no longer trapped in old sin patterns; we belong to a new family. God himself is working in us and polishing us into a reflection of his grace.

The miracle that takes place in the spiritual condition of Christ-followers is so dramatic that we are called new creations in 2 Corinthians 5:17. Our hearts have been changed, and they continue to be changed. Spiritual maturity is an ongoing journey of living out the transformation of our hearts. With humility and dependence on God's Spirit living within us, those changes can and do happen.

How does this happen? We can only answer this question by looking at the example of Jesus in Scripture. Among other passages, Philippians 2:5–11 reveals that his unique inheritance was one of power and authority. Yet, though he had the nature of God, he confined himself to the limits of flesh. Going further, he took on the nature of a servant. Further still, he allowed himself to be executed by the most painful and degrading means known at the time. He humbled himself and gave himself up in love for others.

Jesus passes on this legacy of humility and sacrificial love. He looks nothing like the pseudo-role models our culture worships: men who use their strength to control others, revealing true weakness; men who use risk-taking courage for selfish gain and the accrual of reassuring possessions, revealing their fear; men whose strutting demand for respect is a smoke screen for an insecure identity.

Whatever our inheritance, the key to transforming our legacy is to follow the path Jesus took. He pursued humility and rejected all that was self-serving. His heart and mind were directed to the care of others. That became his legacy. That can be ours as well.

Men who use their strength and courage for others focus on faithfulness, dependability, compassion, and sacrifice. The direction of all these attributes is outward—toward others. None of them are self-directed. The man who pours himself out pours a Christ-like legacy into the lives of everyone he touches.

The transformation of an inheritance of woundedness into a legacy of blessing is not a result of performing and striving. It's a result of brokenness. It's coming to the end of myself and confessing, "If it's up to me to work harder, strive more, and perform better, it's just not going to happen." It's realizing, "Lord, I need you to transform me." The miracle of God's grace is that he actually does!

TRANSFORMATION DETERMINES LEGACY

If we want to repeat the wounds of our inheritance, we can do that on our own. We can pass on anger, fear, weakness, and selfishness naturally and without any effort. In fact, it's because we make no effort that these qualities do get passed on. But if we want a godly legacy, we must pursue genuine community. We need relationships where we tell each other the truth and "spur one another toward love and good deeds" (Hebrews 10:24), where we believe the best of each other and cheer each other on. That's where transformation takes place.

One of the greatest lies men believe is, "I'm the only one who feels what I feel, the only one who struggles with what I am tempted by." I used to believe that my fears and flaws were unique. No one else struggled with them. It has taken a while, but I have come to realize that belief is a lie.

We men need a safe place to share the truth about ourselves because we all struggle with the same issues. We need men who are willing to listen to us, identify with us, and not judge us. We need brothers.

Proverbs 27:17 says, "As iron sharpens iron, so one man sharpens another" (NIV '84). Each scrapes off the corrosion from the other, making both brighter and sharper. Without the interaction and support of other men, we deal with our pain and anger the way we always have:

- We become controlling and destructive in our family relationships.
- We comfort ourselves with alcohol and drugs, sexual fantasy and acting out self-gratification.
- We identify ourselves by the success and affirmation of the workplace.
- We withdraw emotionally and become passive.

We are familiar with these patterns. They are part of the inheritance and legacy of many men. We see them in other men; they see them in us.

Over the years I've been in numerous men's groups. Some have been for mentoring others, or for building community in a church, or for support in my own walk as a man who longs to become more Christ-like. Some have consisted of young men new to the faith, while my current group is made up of four men with over 200 years' of combined experience walking with the Lord. I have learned never to be surprised at what may come to the surface as a man trusts his story with the group. I have also learned that it is often at that precise moment of truth and trust when transformation begins.

In choosing what to call my ministry to men, I was drawn to the name "Peregrine" because the peregrine falcon is the fastest creature designed by God. It's capable of flying at speeds of 200 miles an hour. It mates for life and defends its nest by blowing other birds of prey out of the air, coming out of nowhere and hitting them like a rocket.

I like all that. But what really sold me on the name Peregrine is that it means "pilgrim" in Latin. That's what I am; that's what we all are—pilgrims. Men on a physical journey with a spiritual destination. We desperately need companions on the journey.

It has been said that in isolation we are known by our *weaknesses*, in community we are known by our *strengths*. The darkness and secrets of isolation reinforce our worst habits; the light of authentic community defeats the power of sin, allows others to support us, and invites them to lean on us.

Our legacy is transformed by the power of community. When we love others enough to enter their lives and humble ourselves enough to allow them to enter ours, we become changed. The depth of that engagement with others determines what kind of legacy we will pass on.

First John 1:7 urges us: "But if we walk in the light, as he is in the light, we have fellowship with one another, and the blood of Jesus, his Son, purifies us from all sin." The act of bringing our story out of the shame of darkness into the light of acceptance brings us into a deeper understanding of the power of Jesus' blood, which purifies and transforms us.

STAMPED WITH THE IMAGE OF GOD

The two most important decisions in life—determining our relationship with Christ and creating our legacy—are rooted in grace. In *Growing in His Image*, a profound reinterpretation of the writings of Thomas à Kempis, Bernard Bangley says this about what is truly important in life:

Human nature wants recognition. It wants admiration for good deeds. But grace hides its good works and private devotion and gives all praise to God. Such grace is a heavenly light, a gift from God. It is the mark of a truly spiritual person. As nature is restrained, grace increases, and the soul becomes stamped with the image of God.

As our nature is restrained, our soul becomes "stamped with the image of God."

In working toward a meaningful legacy, we must allow God to

transform us; otherwise we will most assuredly pass on the same self-centered convictions and wounds of the inheritance we received. The truly significant life is not about wealth, admiration, or status. It is about grace, compassion, and forgiveness. It is about community, servanthood, and courage. These are the attributes that define a legacy that will live forever; all of them are for the benefit of others.

QUESTIONS
FOR FURTHER THOUGHT OR DISCUSSION

1. How would you describe the legacy your parents passed on to you and your siblings? What are the primary ways they have impacted others in the family, the workplace, the church, the community?

2. How much thought have you put into comparing what they passed on to what you want to pass on? In what ways do you want to follow their example? In what ways do you want to pass on a different kind of legacy?

3. If you're married, how was your wife's "family inheritance" different from yours? Does hers look more like blessing or more like damage? Have you specifically talked about changes you both want to make in what you pass on to others?

4. What next step will it take for you to make those changes?

CHAPTER 9

YOUR LEGACY TO MEN

During the throes of the Cold War in the late 1970s, Beryl and I were driving a European Ford Transit van through a region of Yugoslavia now called Slovenia. As we approached the border with Austria—the border between Communism and freedom—we found ourselves in a long line of vehicles waiting for passport and customs checks before being allowed out of the country and into the West.

A man in a suit and trench coat walked out of the border station, past the twelve vehicles in front of us and strolled up to the driver's side window of our van. Being singled out in this way was alarming to say the least. He did not wear a uniform and appeared to be unarmed, but his demeanor made it clear that he was in charge and that any of several nearby guards with AK-47s were at his disposal should trouble arise.

He looked like a Serbo-Croatian version of Columbo, the rumpled, disheveled, but extremely sharp detective who became such a popular character on American TV. But the effect was not comical. This agent gave the distinct impression that underestimating him or trying to outsmart him would be a big mistake.

"Columbo" signaled me to roll down the window. "Give me your passports," he ordered. "Pull your van over to the right, park it, take everything out of the back, and lay it on the ground. Don't move. Wait until I get back."

The words were spoken in excellent English. Under other circumstances this might have been a welcome taste of home, but now it only added to the chilling sense that this guy was savvy, well-educated, and a formidable threat.

Being ordered to empty the contents of our van would have been upsetting even if we were ordinary tourists, but we were not tourists. We had just delivered a forbidden cargo of Christian books to a pastor near the town of Novi Sad in the Serbian region. The pastor in turn had just printed several stacks of Christian newsletters and had asked us to deliver those equally forbidden leaflets to churches in Bratislava, Czechoslovakia (now Slovakia). In other words, Beryl and I were smugglers.

On the contraband scale, Bibles and Christian literature are not in the same league as drugs, guns, or state secrets, but in Communist Yugoslavia back then, as in some parts of the world even today, being caught bringing Christian material into a country where Christianity was restricted or banned could result in prison sentences of several years.

What made this border stop even more alarming was that we had just completed our main assignment, smuggling Christian books *into* Yugoslavia. We would have preferred some time to savor the relief of having finished that project. We didn't relish the idea of bringing more literature across the Yugoslav-Austrian border, but we had cheerfully agreed to take the newsletters back with us. This, after all, was why we were in Europe to begin with, to carry the light of the Gospel into countries where it was banned, and to bring comfort, encouragement, and community to Christians who felt isolated from the rest of the world.

Now we were being detained with this contraband, just a few hundred yards from the Austrian border and freedom. Not only might we be arrested, but the pastor who wrote the newsletters might be swept up and imprisoned as well.

Perhaps during our four years as smugglers, we had become too comfortable in the routine. Never before had we seen an agent pass every other vehicle in line, single us out, and tell us to empty our vehicle. As he walked back to the guard station, we wrestled with our predicament. Ignore him and leave everything inside the van and our lack of cooperation might land us in jail. Obey him and he would plainly see that we were the smugglers he apparently suspected we were.

As a husband, I struggled with even more than that. Yes, Beryl and I had undergone the same rigorous mission training. We both understood we were signing up to be smugglers—that is, criminals—but after careful thought and prayer we had decided that sharing the gospel was never a crime. We both understood the risks and had freely decided to take them on.

But the reality of our situation was being driven home to me: the prospect of jail time, of my wife being imprisoned in a foreign country, of being separated from each other and our families and friends, perhaps for months or years. Why on earth had I led her into this peril? How did we get here? How would we get home?

EARLY HEROES

When I was a boy I loved reading about heroes. Some were real life characters such as Kit Carson, Patrick Henry, and Francis Marion, "The Swamp Fox." These men lived beyond the scope of ordinary humans in the ways they changed the world and were immortalized for it.

Other heroes I read about were from a fantasy world: The Man of Steel, The Flash, and Batman. I loved how "The Caped Crusader" remained virtually unseen in his Bat Cave. Unseen, that is, until some bad guy needed to get his butt kicked.

The Crusader responded to the Bat signal on the clouds above Gotham City. In short time, deserving butts were righteously kicked, justice was restored, and Batman returned to his lair. Something about that recurring theme of wrongs being corrected, of those living in fear once again knowing peace, drew my imagination.

As I grew older, through the 1960s and 70s, I was drawn to books about the Cold War. One of my favorites was *The Spy Who Came in from the Cold*, written by John LeCarre in 1963. It described the story of a career spy, always looking over his shoulder, covering his tracks, never knowing whom to trust, always pulling away from relationships before they became too close. Eventually the spy had to find relief from his misery and solitude, retiring from the game. He "came in from the cold."

The darkness and mysterious quality of that phrase, "coming in from the cold," has always intrigued me. It sparked my interest in the Cold War and the people living in the Soviet bloc.

When I was about 20 I read a book about a genuine hero. It was called *God's Smuggler*, written by a man with the pseudonym, Brother Andrew. It described his exploits bringing Bibles and other Christian literature to believers living behind the Iron Curtain.

I was fascinated by the risks Brother Andrew took and by the courage of the Eastern European Christians who valued their faith above their own safety. I marveled at the miracles God performed, blinding the eyes of border guards, allowing loads of literature to get past machine-gun-armed soldiers. This man and his colleagues were modern day heroes!

MINISTRY ON OUR TERMS

A few years after reading *God's Smuggler*, Beryl and I decided to spend a year after college with a short-term missions team. Kevin Dyer, the founder and director of what was then called Literature Crusades, told us of two options. One was Bangladesh. Just about anyone alive in the mid-70s remembers the horrors that nation was experiencing: warfare, famine, disease, poverty, and typhoons. Conditions were so awful that George Harrison of the Beatles initiated one of the first rock "Aid" concerts to draw attention to the conditions in Bangladesh and to raise funds for its suffering citizens.

Honestly, this was a stretch beyond anything we imagined getting ourselves into. We were thinking one year, probably Europe, see the sights, do something significant, then return to "real life." We didn't want to get too carried away by this mission thing.

Our reply to Kevin was, "Could you tell us a little about the second option?" It was to join a team smuggling Bibles behind the Iron Curtain. Images of the heroic Brother Andrew came immediately to mind. Now that, we thought, we can do.

It didn't take long for us to decide that this was the direction we wanted to go.

It changed our lives. First came nine months of pre-field training, which we agreed to only because it was required before joining the team in Vienna.

Those nine months led to our first year overseas, during which we were powerfully confronted by the Holy Spirit through the words of George Verwer, the founder and director of Operation Mobilization. After hearing George speak at a conference in Belgium in 1977, Beryl and I were so pierced at the selfishness of our attitudes that we walked back to our dorm, fell to our knees, and wept. We confessed to God our pride, our self-centeredness, and our insistence on living life on our terms.

Through tears we prayed, "Lord, forgive us for trying to control our lives. We release our plans, our possessions back in the States, our dreams of what the future looks like. We let it go, Lord. You lead us."

Having released our own timetable, we quickly went through our one-year plan barrier. For more than four years we traveled throughout Eastern Europe bringing Christian literature to believers and churches living in oppression and fear. What Beryl and I discovered through this experience was that the real heroes were those believers who demonstrated incredible courage by receiving and distributing literature for others in their churches or neighborhoods.

We also discovered that God could protect us when we felt most vulnerable, which brings us back to that frightening encounter with "Columbo," the police agent at the border of Maribor, Yugoslavia.

Though we often used specialized vehicles with secret compartments in the fenders, walls, and floors in which we hid literature, our Ford Transit was not one of those vehicles. It had a front seat and an empty compartment behind it with benches on the sides on which we'd lay a few boards to make a bed for the night.

We had put the newsletters in two stacks, covered them with newspaper and laid them under the benches. We had packed food boxes, sleeping bags, blankets, and suitcases in front of the stacks and prayed they would never be seen.

But now the border agent had ordered everything unloaded. After quick conversation and whispered prayers for wisdom and protection, we pulled our clothes, food, and bags out of the back and stacked them in a pile on the ground. But we left the literature under the benches. It was moderately out of sight, but still visible to anyone who stepped into the van. We locked the back door, stood by our belongings, and waited.

Columbo returned a few minutes later with a German shepherd on a leash. This couldn't be good. If the armed guards hadn't already eliminated the possibility of us making a run for the border, the thought of being chased by an attack dog kept us frozen in place.

First, the dog sniffed our shoes and pants. Next, the highly disciplined animal sniffed around our luggage, under the wheel wells, all the way around the van, and was not even distracted by the food we had packed. The agent even took the dog into the front seat and had him sniff under the dashboard.

Beryl and I silently prayed, "Lord, please don't let him go in back." If he did, there was no way he'd miss the literature. Our hearts sank as the agent eventually turned to me and said, "Unlock the back door." I did and he led the dog inside. We knew we were caught.

We watched helplessly as the agent pointed along the right-side floor where it met the sidewalls under the bench and walked forward. The dog sniffed wherever he pointed. Finally, he came to the stack of material behind the front seat, looked at it, and pointed. The dog sniffed the stack of newsletters. We waited breathlessly, wondering if we would be handcuffed and marched away.

But that did not happen. Instead, to our amazement, the detective and his dog pivoted to the left side of the van and the other stack of Christian newsletters. He had the dog sniff that stack, then pulled him along the left wall until he came to the rear door.

Finally, Colombo and the dog hopped out and he commanded, "Get all this inside and get back in line." With that he turned and led his dog back to the station.

Beryl and I stood dumbfounded. What had happened? Was he blind? Were we safe, or were we just going to "get it" when we pulled to the front of the line?

Thirty agonizing minutes later, we reached the head of the line. Columbo was nowhere to be seen. A uniformed guard handed us our passports, gave one last skeptical look through my window into the back compartment, and in heavily accented English simply said, "Go."

We never celebrated an entry to the green grass, rolling hills, and blue skies of Austria more than on that day. Of course, the colors weren't that much different from the landscape behind the Iron Curtain, but compared to the gray, somber, hopeless lifestyle of those in Communist countries, everything in the West looked and smelled better.

Not until we arrived in Vienna that night did we fully understand our encounter with Columbo. The news was filled with the story of a cache of heroin found the day before at that very same border in the same style of Ford Transit van with Dutch registered plates just like ours. It had been the largest load of drugs ever captured at that border.

To the embarrassment of the Yugoslavs, however, they had missed it. It was caught on the Austrian side of the border. It was a political scandal for Yugoslav security and they were determined it would never happen again. That's why we were singled out. That's why a detective and not a regular guard came to our van. That's why he brought a dog, trusting its nose rather than his own eyes. And that's why we made it safely out of the country.

TIRED, CONFUSED, AND ALONE

But God didn't choose to protect the "God smugglers" all the time. Not every trip was successful.

One of those I had the privilege to work alongside for a few years was a young man from Finland I'll call Aleks. He was a physical, mental, and spiritual specimen. He was 6'2", carried 185 pounds of muscle and zero fat. He was on the Finnish Jr. National Hockey Team. Playing soccer against him was an exercise in futility. He could outrun you while dribbling, fake you out of your shorts, or just run right over you.

Aleks was also deeply committed to his relationship with God, spending hours every week reading Scripture, journaling, and praying. He was a unique young man, physically and spiritually powerful.

In December 1979, Aleks, who lived in Vienna and studied fulltime at the University of Vienna, went on a trip, smuggling 100 Bibles into the Soviet Union. For all of us in the ministry at that time, a trip into the Soviet Union was the Major Leagues. All the Soviet bloc countries were difficult and frightening to travel into with Christian literature. We had to be prepared for tough checks and the possibility of interrogation and imprisonment.

Czechoslovakia, Romania, and Bulgaria were tough, but nothing compared with the intense border checks and surveillance of the Soviet Union. The Soviet guards had no concern for how they treated you, how much time they took to examine your personal articles, or what kind of damage they did to your vehicle in their pursuit of "guns, drugs, pornography, or Bibles."

Only small, very well-concealed loads of literature had any chance of getting through. But if anyone could do it, Aleks could. He was deeply committed and courageous.

Aleks' fateful trip began one evening after he'd finished his comprehensive mid-term finals. He traveled alone. His plan was to go through Moscow, drop off his contraband Bibles with a known Christian contact and make his way home to Finland for Christmas break. That's not what happened.

Arriving late at night at a nearly deserted border station, Aleks' car was taken into a garage, torn apart piece by piece and, after several hours, the Bibles discovered and confiscated. He was immediately jailed and submitted to interrogation by the secret police.

A month later Aleks returned to Vienna and we had coffee together. He trusted me with a story he was deeply ashamed of. Within 24 hours of his arrival at the Soviet border, under ruthless interrogation, he broke. He answered every question the authorities asked him. He told everything he knew about the work operating out of Austria. He even told them who he knew and what our nationalities were.

Fortunately, most of us were known only by code names so he was not able to divulge our real names. He only knew me as Peter. He told me that if he had known my real name he would have given it up. I couldn't imagine the pressure that would have caused Aleks to break like that.

Once the authorities knew they had everything Aleks could tell them they let him go on to Finland. They broke his will in less than a day. Unbelievable!

"Aleks," I said, "you're one of the toughest men physically, spiritually, and emotionally I know. How were they able to get to you?"

This is what he told me, "Peter, when I left for my trip I had just completed a week of intense study and days of final exams. I was drained. When the secret police interrogated me they kept me awake, they accused me of undermining their State. They said God would be ashamed of my actions. They got me to doubt myself and doubt God. Peter, I was tired, confused, and alone. That's all it took for me to break."

Tired, confused, and alone. That describes many men I know.

Replacing Tiredness with Encouragement

Perhaps it describes you. You are putting in long hours at work, perhaps 50, 60, or 70 hours a week. You have little time to invest in relationships, in recreation or in rest. You long for a schedule that allows balance in the areas of life that are important to you, but you can't get your head above water.

Or perhaps your career is depleting you. You have settled into a rut that is all-too familiar. It brings in an income and keeps you off the streets, but it's uninspiring and mind numbing. You long for a meaningful vocation that truly takes advantage of your gifts and passion. You regularly ask yourself, "Really? Is this it for the rest of my life?"

Or your home life is running you ragged. Your relationships with family, friends, and neighbors are stretching you beyond your ability to handle the challenges.

You are absolutely *tired*.

If this describes you, you're not the only one. You need support; you need to come in from the cold of tiredness. You need to find community with a group of like-minded men who can help replace your *tiredness* with *encouragement*.

Hebrews 10:24–25 tells us to, "Spur one another on to love and good deeds, not giving up meeting together, as some are in the habit of doing, but encouraging one another—and all the more as you see the Day approaching." We are literally to be cheerleaders for one another, believing the best of each other, reminding one another what our values and priorities truly are, and holding us to them.

Several years ago I led a small group of men who didn't know each other. They came together because they were overwhelmed with the challenges life was throwing at them. They were tired and they needed encouragement. Early on, the prayer requests shared at the end of our study were typically safe: Aunt Harriet fell and broke her pelvis; my son has a baseball try-out today; my wife has a dental appointment. The requests were about other people; these men didn't reveal a thing about their own lives.

Then one day a man asked for prayer for an upcoming business trip to LA: safe flight, protection for the family while he was gone, ideas for how to save more money as a company. Same old safe stuff. Then he paused, thought for a moment, and said, "And pray that when the rest of the guys go to a strip club I'll have the courage to say no. This time."

I wanted to jump up and cheer! He had just crossed a line. He spoke a deeper, more courageous truth about his life. I wondered how the others would respond.

Finally, one man said, "I'll pray for you. I was in a strip club in Vegas last week." After his prayer, we talked about this topic further and eventually five of the eight men admitted that they struggled with the same temptation.

The men in that group had just come in from the cold. And they discovered that together they could provide strength and encouragement for one another.

Men, many of us are tired of the battle constantly raging around us. We desperately need to spur one another on to love and good deeds. We need encouragement. And for that, we need to be connected with other men with whom we can share the deeper truths about our lives.

REPLACING CONFUSION WITH CLARITY

Perhaps you are wondering whether others struggle with the same issues you do. You are questioning your faith or whether God is paying attention to the fears that keep you awake at night. You have constant challenges at work that require an ethical stance on your part, and sometimes you have no idea which way to go.

Or perhaps you face demanding decisions that affect your marriage or children and the consequences seem increasingly monumental.

You are completely *confused*.

If this describes you, you're not the only one. You need to find some like-minded men who can help you come in from the cold of *confusion* and find *clarity*.

The book of Proverbs urges us all to seek wisdom from God and to invite the counsel of others. Proverbs 12:15 says, "The way of fools seems right to them, but the wise listen to advice." Later on, verse 15:22 tells us, "Plans fail for lack of counsel, but with many advisors they succeed."

Men, we need to rely on others when we are confused.

A few years ago I left a job that I had poured my heart into, but felt like I had failed in. For months afterward I pursued job opportunities, but there was always something missing in the options that came my way. I seriously considered a complete change of careers, but encountered uncertainty and confusion in my thinking. As my transition pay package was coming to an end I needed to find a solution, but I felt lost and God wasn't speaking very clearly. In fact, I couldn't hear him at all.

I did the only thing I knew to do. I called men in my small group and asked them to come to my home that evening. They cleared their schedules and came to my support. They listened to my pain and fear. We prayed, we wept, and they reminded me of the truth of God's care and his power to provide for my family and me.

They helped me come in from the cold of confusion.

Many of us men struggle with the complexity of the problems we face in life. When we are struggling with confusion we need the counsel and advice of godly men who can help us find clarity. For that we need to be connected with other men.

REPLACING ISOLATION WITH COMMUNITY

Perhaps you face the challenges of each day with a gnawing sense of isolation. You are aware of the fact that no one knows the real you, and you're not sure what they would think if they did. You are around people every day, but couldn't honestly call them friends.

Your wife cares about you, but she has no idea exactly what you have to deal with on a daily basis. Your kids can't even tell their friends what kind of work you do. You're *alone*.

If this describes you, you're not the only one. You need to come in from the cold of *isolation* and into *community*.

Scripture warns us against attempting our spiritual journey on our own. Proverbs 21:6 says, "A man who strays from the path of understanding comes to rest in the company of the dead." Elsewhere we are encouraged that whenever two or three or more of us come together, God himself is in the middle of that gathering (Matthew 18:20).

A couple of years ago I met a man I'll call Tom. He was in a small group of men, but had dropped out and not met with the others for several weeks. During that time the marriage issues he had been struggling with for many months became worse. Without the support and accountability of his friends he remained in isolation. Predictably, the problems he had at home and work spiraled out of control.

Over time we in the group heard he had left his wife, family, and job and had moved in with a woman in another state. Months passed before Tom gave me a call out of the blue and asked if we could get together. I could hardly believe my eyes due to the physical condition Tom was in—gaunt, skinny, long straggling hair, tattoos, pins and needles in his skin. I was horrified to hear that Tom had lapsed into suicidal depression.

One night, Tom bought a bottle of whiskey and a long, thick rope. He ran the rope from the driver's seat of his hatchback car through the back and tied it around the concrete base of a street light in a parking lot. He got in the driver's seat and tied the other end of the rope into a noose and put it around his neck. His plan was to take courage from his last companion, Jack Daniels, drain the bottle, tighten the noose, buckle the seat belt, start the car, and roar off at full speed. In a few brief seconds his troubles would be over.

Thankfully, before completing his mission, Tom passed out from the alcohol. He woke up the next morning half in the car, half on the ground. His plot had failed and he lived to tell the story.

In isolation Tom was overwhelmed with shame and self-condemnation and nearly killed himself. He needed to return to the fellowship of men who cared about him, to hear their counsel and prayers, to regain a balanced view of his options—none of which included suicide.

"A man who strays from the path of understanding comes to rest in the company of the dead." Tom came unbelievably close to fulfilling that verse. While his story may seem extreme, the reality is that many men live lives of dark isolation. We fight our battles in silence. We hide secrets that only gain greater strength in the darkness of loneliness.

We desperately need to allow ourselves to be drawn out of isolation and into community.

REAL HEROES

Earlier I mentioned that many of my boyhood heroes were fantastic characters like Superman, Batman, and The Flash. But they weren't real men. A real man, a real hero, is someone who knows he needs others in his life. He takes the risk of:
- Revealing the truth about himself to others
- Caring about others
- Relying on others
- Focusing on the needs of others

That's a true hero:

- A *tired* man who pursues *encouragement*
- A *confused* man who pursues *clarity*
- An *isolated* man who pursues *community*

He's a man who knows it's time to finally come in from the cold. He pursues connection with other men.

Aleks and countless millions of men like him find that there is a limit to their strength. I suspect that at some point in your life you have encountered the same sobering truth. If you haven't, you will.

How much more exhaustion will it take for you to reach out for the encouragement available from other men?

How much more confusion will you live with before you ask others to help you find clarity?

How lonely will you let yourself get before you climb out of your cave and let a trusted friend know you want community? Yes, it takes courage and humility to step toward another man, but you have it in you.

When I had that stunning conversation with Aleks after his disastrous Bible smuggling trip, he had piercing clarity about what had happened to cause his downfall. In retrospect he knew he was too tired, too confused, and too isolated for the battle he entered into. He would have given anything to rewind the tape and do it again.

You can learn from Aleks' story and reach out to one, two, or three men you want to trust.

This week. Come in from the cold.

You can do it!

QUESTIONS
FOR FURTHER THOUGHT OR DISCUSSION

1. What has been your experience in trying to reach out to, or trust, men: In your family, at work, at church, in the community?

2. The Bible smuggler who broke under interrogation did so because he was "tired, confused and alone." In what ways are you:

- Tired: drained, fed up, at your limit, physically and emotionally stretched?

- Confused: facing complicated issues, hearing two sides of a story that don't fit, needing to make a major decision but the right choice is unclear, just plain lost?

- Alone: perhaps not literally friendless, but feeling alone in facing the life-demands you deal with all the time?

3. Do you have a group of friends you can go to for support? What can you and your group do to make your connections deeper, more genuine and life-giving?

CHAPTER 10

YOUR LEGACY TO WOMEN

As we consider the legacy men are to pass on to others, perhaps none is more important than the legacy we leave with women. From the very beginning God gave the first man a woman to bring partnership, joy, and completion to his life.

Women still bring the same profound gifts into the lives of men. The women in our lives indescribably enrich our world. In the same way we should be an enriching presence in their lives. But we know it's not as easy as it sounds. We know there are plenty of differences between men and women. Marriage offers numerous opportunities to discover countless nuances; those nuances often lead to conflict.

Here are a few key insights for understanding women I heard from an anonymous, wise source. For men who are already married, this may give new insight into your experience. For those who are not, this will give you an idea of the mystery your brothers live with:

- A man will pay $2 for a $1 item he needs; a woman will pay $1 for a $2 item she doesn't need at all.
- A woman worries about the future until she gets a husband; a man never worries about the future…until he gets a wife.

- To be happy with a man, you must understand him a lot and love him a little; to be happy with a woman, you must love her a lot... and not try to understand her...*at all.*
- A woman has the last word in any argument; anything a man says after that is the beginning of the *next* argument.

The differences between men and women humorously illustrated in the above list arise in most male/female relationships. The relationship of marriage in particular brings unlimited opportunities for misunderstanding, conflict, insight, and growth.

Marriage can seem attractive to those who are unmarried and a struggle for those who are married. Someone made the observation, "Marriage is like flies on a screen door. Those on the outside want in; those on the inside want out."

This year Beryl and I celebrated our 41st anniversary. She is literally the greatest earthly gift God has ever given me. When it comes to marriage, I recommend it. Highly. But I don't intend this chapter to be solely a marriage primer. In fact, my comments will apply to a man's relationship with women even if he's not married. I want to cast a broader vision and lay a foundation for what I believe is God's design for how men and women best complete one another.

What I'll mention is controversial. In recent decades we have seen a dramatic change in views on how men and women relate. Those changes have impacted every realm of society: business, community, church, and family.

Let me preface this by saying I'm on a journey of understanding the roles of men and women myself. I grew up in a very conservative church background. When in the church, the women were expected to remain silent. They wore head coverings to demonstrate their submission to men in general and their husbands in particular. Women were to be meek and submissive. Men were understood to be the leaders in the marriage, family, and church.

This approach, intentionally or not, taught an attitude of gender hierarchy—not just that men were to lead, but that they were spiritually superior and that women were inferior. I'm married to a talented, gifted, strong-minded woman. She wanted nothing to do with head coverings. I loved that about her. She demonstrates her love and respect for me in countless ways that matter much more to me than what she's got on her head.

Over the years as Beryl and I have lived overseas and in a few states, I've seen a broad spectrum of Christian beliefs and practices when it comes to the role of women. I've been on staff at a large Evangelical church that encouraged women to serve as teachers, leaders, and elders. The difference there from what I grew up in could hardly have been more dramatic.

I know what I believe today and I hold to it with conviction. But I also realize I am on a journey of understanding that continues to unfold. That journey may well take me beyond my current perspective. I hold my understanding with an open hand, just in case God decides to reveal more.

What I say may seem controversial, but my intent is not to shock. I dislike grandstanding through words. But at the same time, I'll state my opinions firmly. My intent is to open your eyes, raise questions, prompt your thinking, and stir your thoughts on God's calling for your relationships with women.

Let's start with a basic question.

ARE MEN NECESSARY?

Men, what will be your legacy to the women in your life, most specifically your wife, if and when you have one?

Debate rages today regarding the roles of husband and wife. It's part of a larger debate mentioned in chapter 1. Other than for the purpose of sperm donation, are men really necessary? Do women and children even need men in the family?

In movies and TV, men, especially fathers, are often portrayed as bumbling idiots who couldn't survive a day without their wives. We may laugh at *The Simpsons, Everybody Loves Raymond, The King of Queens, Family Guy,* or *Modern Family,* but ultimately we are watching examples of men who are often ridiculed or ignored by their kids and whose wives carry all the meaningful parental authority in the family. I don't know anyone who aspires to be that kind of man.

Does our society need men? If so, what is our role with women in our society supposed to be? The answer is revealed by how God has designed us as men. Our calling can be summed up this way: Men are to love women by taking initiative to ensure they are valued, protected, respected, and unleashed. Men are to give their lives to women so they in turn have abundant life.

I believe it is God's design for men to lead self-sacrificially in our relationships with women, especially in marriage, for three reasons:

1. Our bodies reveal God's design. If you want to know what the heart of a man looks like, one clue is between his legs. The same is true of a woman's heart. I say this with utmost sincerity and respect for God's creation, and without any intent of crude humor. Our anatomy reflects the design of our hearts and the way we best relate as man and woman. Christian authors Larry Crabb, John Eldredge and others have written on this subject.

"Men are the pointed ones," I heard Crabb shockingly say many years ago at a conference in Colorado. I had never heard it put this way before! Our physical design is different on purpose. It is not just a happy consequence of natural selection.

A man's genitals point and extend; a woman's don't. As we men are physically "pointed," so are we created to relate to our world. We are to lead, extend, move into, and point the way.

The differences between men and women are not only physical; they are also psychological and spiritual. A man's heart and soul is most clearly demonstrated through the most intimate aspect possible of a male-female relationship: intercourse. Eldredge says, not very subtly, that in sex "the man rises to the occasion."

You get the picture. God designed men to be action-oriented:
- When stirred, man rises
- He leads and points the way

- He enters into the life of others; most intimately, his wife's
- He does so with passion, firmness, and tenderness—and he empties himself of everything he has
- The result brings fulfillment, joy, and life to others

A woman's heart and soul is also reflected through her body's design and is most clearly demonstrated through intercourse. She receives and makes herself available and vulnerable. Women are the open ones. God designed women to be strongly connection-oriented:

- She opens herself up and becomes vulnerable, physically and emotionally
- She allows her husband to enter into her deepest, most sensitive being
- She welcomes him into her life; she surrounds him and accepts him
- The result brings fulfillment, joy and life to others

This is not just pure luck. This is God's design. It matters deeply and it is filled with meaning for how we relate to each other outside of sex. God made the souls and the bodies of men and women to be different and yet perfectly compatible in order to give to, and bring out, the best in each other.

When it works, we experience the greatest thrills and deepest emotions of life. Emotions that are impossible without each other. The end result is joy, connection, and life.

God designed men and women to fill different sexual roles. It only makes sense that we would also be designed different emotionally. The tendencies of male and female souls is a demonstration that the man is called to take initiative by entering into the life of the woman he loves. I believe he is also to be the primary initiator in marriage. That takes courage, compassion, and intention.

Not long ago I talked over coffee with three friends about our family circumstances. Each of us revealed an area where we were working to find the motivation and courage to re-enter the lives of our wives, to engage once again on tired issues. The topics seem to repeat themselves. We see progress some days and discouragement on others. We have a tendency to want to rise up and control or intimidate, or else to withdraw and stand on the sideline.

These extremes are easier paths than the one requiring us to love, to take initiative, to humble ourselves, to risk being misunderstood, to be wrong or confused. To risk requires courage. The mere act of noticing, entering, and seeking resolution tells our wives they are worth pursuing.

Men, our bodies reveal God's design. We are the pointed ones; we are to take action toward our wives and lead with both strength and tenderness. Obviously the sexual aspect of this metaphor should be acted out *only* with our wives but there is a sense in which men should engage with all women courageously and compassionately.

2. Our hearts reveal God's design. There is something deep in the heart of a man that wants to lead, defend, and serve the love of his life.

This is a consistent theme throughout literature, art, and culture all over the world throughout history. The stories that stir men *and* many women are stories of a man who uses his strength and courage for the benefit of the woman of his dreams.

Movie epics like *Braveheart, Dances with Wolves, Last of the Mohicans, Gladiator, Titanic, Inception, Mission: Impossible, Iron Man, Captain America,* all demonstrate a man fighting on behalf of a woman he loves as a central theme. Not coincidentally, they usually include a woman trusting a courageous, self-sacrificial man.

Anyone who has raised a daughter can testify that most girls grow up with visions of someday being swept off their feet by a man, who, though powerful, is tender and trustworthy. As an adult, that girl will still deeply long for a man to whom she can entrust herself with abandon, without any fear of harm or shame.

My granddaughters are completely captivated by the princesses who have appeared in stories both recent and historic: Sleeping Beauty, Snow White, Rapunzel, Anna and Elsa in *Frozen*, and Cinderella. Most of those stories include a Prince Charming with whom the main character falls in love. He is courageous, faithful, strong, and captivated by the beauty and grace of the "princess."

Girls who dream of a Prince Charming become women who hold on to the same hope for a strong yet trustworthy man.

Sadly, though many men are wonderfully trustworthy, all of us are fallen and have our own selfish desires. As a result we inflict pain on the very women who dare to make themselves vulnerable with us. We take advantage of them in order to meet our own needs or to soothe our own wounds.

Over the past decades the traditional roles of men and women have been challenged—initially through the women's liberation movement, and then in virtually every setting where men and women relate: family, work, athletics, and even church.

Much of this re-evaluation of roles has been healthy and necessary. As I look back at the TV stereotypes of women in the 50s and 60s, I can hardly believe them. I recall the June Cleavers and Harriet Nelsons of TV land; their primary jobs were to cook, vacuum, and clean, all while wearing dresses, pearl necklaces, and perfect make-up. When Ward Cleaver or Ozzie Nelson showed up, his wife knew her job was to get him the newspaper, slippers, and pipe.

As much as Beryl loves me and genuinely respects me, that's not exactly the way she welcomes me home. In fact, since I work out of an office in my home, it is *I* who am usually welcoming *her* home. In neither case are the newspaper, slippers, and a pipe involved.

Many of our churches also treated women in ways that left them feeling unvalued, ungifted, and of lesser importance than men. My own church background non-verbally communicated to women that they were spiritually inferior. In essence women were told, "Be quiet, cover up, submit."

Sometimes women who experience the harshness and condescension of this kind of approach respond in ways that reveal their resulting wounds. We may notice a subtle edginess in tone or attitude; a driven energy to perform and excel. Perhaps a woman will reveal a sharp edge that's especially reflected in any discussion about male/female roles at work or church.

We need to recognize that so many women have suffered spiritual wounds from condescending male spiritual-authority figures. (Similarly, I've seen in many men from legalistic churches our *own* set of wounds coming from expectations placed on us. Myself included.)

Because of the wounds inflicted on them by men, some women have a very hard time trusting and submitting to any man. Once we hear their stories, that distrust makes enormous sense. What if we were the kind of men who regained their trust?

There is a message in our hearts convicting us that a man's impact is deep. But it can be used for either blessing or destruction. It's a message that says a man is most manly when his strength is disciplined, and when women can fully trust his leadership. They can trust him because they are convinced his strength will be used for their own good.

It's a message telling us that a woman is most womanly when she respects her man enough to trust him, to relax, and to let her inner gift—strength, perceptiveness, beauty—flourish in partnership with a man who would literally die for her.

Unfortunately, men's leadership is often anything but loving or sacrificial; it is far too often destructive and selfish. As a result, women often learn that it's not safe to trust, and they pull away or wreak their own angry damage on their partners.

Too often we both fail one another. How tragic.

When I co-led a men's ministry in one church, I frequently encountered the challenge of calling men to step into a more Christ-like leadership role in their homes, while at the same time worshipping in an environment that strongly encouraged women to exercise their gifts, including leadership gifts, without regard to gender.

Many of the women in leadership roles in that church are some of the most gifted and godly people I've ever met. But, ironically, the very practice of de-emphasizing gender distinctions in deploying spiritual gifts tended to de-emphasize the very gender-uniqueness that my colleagues and I were trying to convey to apathetic, disengaged, and passive men.

I often wondered what some of those very gifted staff women felt about the roles I was encouraging men to fill with their wives. So, one day I asked a staff woman whom I deeply respected. She was a gifted teacher, perceptive mentor of men and women, and one of the most respected ministry leaders in the church.

"Sue," I asked, "Scripture seems to say, and my experience tells me, that a marriage works best if the husband takes a self-sacrificing leadership role. His wife contributes her own gifts and leadership skills as well, ultimately respecting her husband by honoring his leadership. Can you tell me your reaction to this idea?"

"Craig," she responded, "I'll tell you a little secret we women have amongst ourselves. We dream of having a man who loves us for who we are, and who leads by sacrificing himself for our benefit. We would *gladly* submit to a man like that."

This from a woman who was extremely fruitful in ministry, highly respected, and the divorced partner of a man who was unfaithful to her. She herself was deeply wounded by the betrayal of a man she trusted, but deep inside she still longed to entrust herself to a good man's leadership.

There is something in our hearts that resonates with what Sue said. She's right; that is the way God intended it. Our experience confirms that men need and want to lead their wives, and their wives need and want to be able to trust and respect the leadership of their husbands. Our hearts reveal God's design that this is the way men and women most naturally relate to one another.

3. Scripture reveals God's design. Ephesians 5:21–28 is one of the most insightful, and at the same time most resented, portrayals of God's intent for husbands and wives. I was once asked to use this passage for my comments in the wedding ceremony of a young couple whose spiritual backgrounds were quite different. She came from a long line of committed Christians. He was the first and only Christ-follower in his family.

I referred to the passage, because the couple asked me to, but didn't spend much time on it. Just enough to point out the truth and promise it holds for men and women committed to each other for life. It happened to be a summer wedding on an extremely humid day in a sanctuary with no air-conditioning.

During the service, one of the bridesmaids suddenly fainted. It was quite a showstopper and we all lent a hand to this woman feeling the combined affects of the heat, humidity, and tension on the most important day in her bride-friend's life.

A few days later I got an email from the groom's uncle. It wasn't a pleasant message: "How dare you take the stage during my nephew's wedding! How dare you take advantage of their important day and fill it with your pompous archaic Bible message. You went on so long with your preaching even the bridesmaids were dropping like flies!"

That struck me as a little over-the-top. I replied by saying if he had a problem with the passage being included in the ceremony he should take it up with the bride and groom. If he had a problem with the content of the passage he needed to take it up with a higher authority.

Modern-day culture bristles at this passage. It sounds too archaic; it reveals distinctions for men and women rather than treating them exactly alike. The claim that the "husband is the head of the wife" and that wives are to "submit to their husbands" sounds offensive to many.

Maybe, like me, you have done some study into the meaning of the phrase "the husband is the head of the wife." I'm not a Bible scholar, but I do want to understand what God is calling me to in my relationship with Beryl.

Better theologians than me stand in complete opposition in their interpretation and application of this passage. A pastor I highly respect thinks this description is a result of the Fall and is contrary to God's perfect design. Another highly respected seminary professor and author believes that it is precisely because of Eve's role in the Fall that man has been placed as the head.

There is no airtight proof for or against these stances. That's why Christians still debate them. But I will say that for me personally, my experience and intuition heavily influence how I interpret these verses.

In my opinion, Scripture shows us God's design for the husband *is* to be the "head" of the wife—meaning his role is to provide authority, covering, and leadership that blesses and preserves the interdependence and unity of the marriage and each partner. This does not imply a superior/inferior relationship; rather, it's a relationship in which *both* partners perform his or her role to respect and serve the other.

The heart's desire of a woman is to entrust herself freely to the man she loves. She wants a man she can look up to and honor. This requires from her courage, vulnerability, and trust. That's what Ephesians says to her: "Wives, submit yourselves to your own husbands [or as verse 33 says, respect your husbands] as you do to the Lord. For the husband is the head of the wife as Christ is the head of the church" (5:22–23).

This is not angry, begrudging surrender. And it certainly isn't meek submission because the husband is always right or without fault. It is, in its essence, an act of obedience and worship to God. "Submit yourselves to your own husbands as you do to the Lord" (v. 22). This is an act that honors God as much as the husband.

Let's face it, this is not natural! A woman must overcome her own tendencies to control, to protect herself, even to undermine her husband. These tendencies go all the way back to Eve's actions in the Garden and are often further intensified by the pain or mistreatment a woman may have already experienced at the hands of men, including her husband.

To respect her husband, a woman needs the supernatural love of Christ flowing through her on a daily basis. Because in himself, he doesn't deserve it.

She also needs a husband who follows God's commands to him: "Husbands, love your wives, just as Christ loved the church and gave himself up for her" (v. 25). A wife can only submit to her husband as God enables her to and as her husband shows this kind of love to her.

Husbands are called to love. Love how? "As Christ loved the church." What did that look like? He humbled himself, he served others, he healed and taught, and in the end, he sacrificed himself for her.

In his book, *The Four Loves*, C.S. Lewis wrote:

The husband is the head of the wife just in so far as he is to her what Christ is to the Church. He is to love her as Christ loved the

Church…and gave his life for her. This headship, then, is most fully embodied not in the husband we should all wish to be but in him whose marriage is most like a crucifixion.

I'm fairly certain that in using this analogy Lewis did not mean a man's marriage ought to look like sheer agony. No, his point is: a man's role in marriage should indisputably demonstrate immense courage and compassion, borne out of deep love for his "bride."

Christ died for those he loved. That's what a noble man does, too. He dies to himself. He loves his wife so deeply that he sacrifices himself for her. God put that longing in our hearts—it's the story that's told in countless movies and epics—and he commands us to live it out.

If we do, our wives will respect us; they will honor us and follow us anywhere. I think that's the way God designed it. Men love women by taking initiative to ensure they are valued, protected, respected, and unleashed. Men give their lives to women, so they in turn bring life to others.

Is that how I love Beryl? Far too often the answer is "No." Is that how you love your wife? To the extent the answer is "No," you need to change that.

THE ORIGINAL MALE SIN

Why don't we do so? It goes back to the story of Adam who, when his wife needed him to truly love her by defending her, by standing between her and the Enemy's attack, remained silent and passive. Eve was the first to sin, but in many respects her husband failed her first.

This is not the place to get into whether the Garden story in Genesis 3:1–7 is literal or metaphorical; either way it teaches some foundational truths. To summarize, it was indeed Eve who was tempted, and it was she who took the first bite, then offered the forbidden fruit to Adam. Prior to her action she had a significant conversation with Satan.

Where was Adam when this was going on? Was he working in the garden? Was it Sunday afternoon and he was watching the Bears and Lions? No, verse 6 says her husband "was with her." As Crabb points out in his book, *The Silence of Adam*, Adam was present, but he was silent. For the first time in history, but certainly not the last, a man failed his woman by remaining passive and silent. And she, in turn, failed him by seizing control.

When confronted by a challenge, Adam remained silent. When his woman needed him to speak up, to defend her, he was passive. Rather than lead, he abdicated. In a very real way the original, quintessential male sin was passivity.

Faced with her husband's uncertainty and disengagement, Eve did what many women still do. She stepped alone into the vacuum and took matters into her own hands. She filled a void Adam should have filled.

There are two deep longings that all men and women have: the need for Relationship (Love) and the need for Significance (Respect).

All women long for love and respect, but typically a woman's deepest desire is for love. As a result her greatest fear, almost always, is abandonment. The loss or withdrawal of love. To avoid this kind of pain she may become controlling of relationships.

Similarly, all men also long for love and respect, but typically a man's greatest desire is for respect. As a result his greatest fear, almost always, is failure. The loss of respect from others. To avoid this kind of pain he may take on an air of intimidation, or conversely, he may simply give up and become passive.

Adam chose to be passive. When he did, Eve protected herself by taking control. Neither one was filling the God-given roles they needed from one another. And so began, I believe, the pattern that men and women have followed ever since.

By God's design men are called to enter into the lives of others—friends, wives, and children—with courage and compassion. But far too often we don't. The sin of men is to fail women by passively giving up on servant leadership.

Women need men who are willing to risk themselves by "getting in the way." That is, men who, when their loved ones are threatened, stand between them and the threat, whatever it may be. Crabb says that the mark of a real man is one who, when confronted with confusion or conflict, steps into it with courage, compassion, and creativity.

The mark of an immature man is to remain silently passive. The mark of a mature man is to get in the way.

Women need to support the courageous, sacrificial leadership of their men. But far too often they don't. The sin of women is to fail their husbands by grabbing their authority. This has become so common that it is almost a classic pattern of marriages: Homer Simpson-like bumbling men, controlled and demeaned by cop-like women.

The world sees this as normal and humorous—and it's neither. It's a sad distortion of God's magnificent design that honors the hearts of both men and women.

THE GREATEST LINE EVER

Believe it or not, I think Spiderman is a pretty good male role model. Roger Ebert called *Spiderman 2* one of the best super-hero movies ever. Why?

Because it revolves around two timeless male themes: A man searching for his calling in life; and a man finding a strong woman who believes in him and brings out the best in him.

In the last two scenes in the movie, Mary Jane, the love of Peter Parker's life, is about to marry a man who is an obvious hero. Meanwhile Peter (Spidey) stands alone in his apartment. Suddenly Mary Jane leaves her hero groom at the altar and races to Peter's apartment, finding him looking dejectedly out the window.

Peter knows he's losing the most wonderful woman he has ever known. Suddenly sensing someone at his open doorway, he turns to see the gorgeous Mary Jane with tears in her eyes. What ensues is one of the most memorable heart-encounters in male-female movie lore.

Mary Jane: "Isn't it time you let someone rescue you?" (I believe in you; let me support you.) "I've always been at your doorway." (I've always been looking for a man to respect. You're him.)

When they fall into each other's arms, Peter suddenly hears sirens and turns toward the open window. People are in harm's way; a vulnerable society needs someone who will get in the way. Peter realizes *this* is his mission after all. But he turns back to Mary Jane and his eyes express the question every man wants to ask a strong woman who has his back: "I'm needed. Are you with me on this?"

Mary Jane smiles coyly and says one of the best lines ever expressed by a woman in film: "Go get 'em, Tiger."

Spidey ecstatically returns her smile, dives out of the window, and swings on his spider silk toward danger, yelling at the top of his lungs.

Men, when a woman looks at us like that, *we will dive out of a window*!!! That look tells a man, "A woman believes in me and respects who I am!"

As the movie closes, the camera returns to Mary Jane at the window. We see in her eyes the strength that comes from knowing who she is as a woman as well as pride in her heroic, self-sacrificing man. But we also see sober recognition that this will not be an easy journey.

For all the nonsense regularly splashed on TV and movie screens, every now and then Hollywood gets it right. Whoever wrote that scene understands the hearts of men and women better than some psychologists and pastors do. It's a great example of a woman being womanly and a man being manly.

When I first saw it, I sat in the theater with tears steaming down my cheeks. Powerful emotions from somewhere on a heart level overflowed unexpectedly to the surface. And it's a flippin' comic book story about a guy in leotards! I wasn't the only one with tears.

Why do we react this way? Because our hearts know the truth when we see it.

Men need women who believe in them, who open up and trust their leadership. Women need men with a calling beyond themselves who stand up and lead by sacrificing themselves.

Men, what will be your legacy to the women in your life, to your wife in particular? Will it be a continuation of the passive pattern initiated by Adam?

We need to ask ourselves: In what ways are we abdicating our role right now? In what ways are we silent when our wives need us to speak, lead, and defend? If we have areas in which we are passive, what action do we need to take?

We need to get in the way.

On the other hand, what about those of us whose leadership is all too forceful? There is nothing sacrificial or safe about it. It's controlling, hurtful, and selfish. We need to imitate Christ who died so others might live. That is the kind of leadership that anyone, man or woman, would love to follow.

In the end, husbands and wives are both called to love and respect each other. But I believe it begins with the man. That's part of what comes with leading. We extend, we point, we move toward. We have to make the first move. If we respectfully love our wives, they will love to respect us.

First Corinthians 13 tells us, "Love always protects, always trusts, always hopes, always perseveres." We can be this kind of man: one who *protects* women's tenderness, *trusts* women's strengths, *hopes* by believing the best in them, and *perseveres* by consistently sacrificing ourselves to bring them life.

This is terrifically hard to do, but with God's strength we *can* be this kind of man and we can have this kind of legacy with the women in our lives.

Go get 'em, Tiger!

QUESTIONS
FOR FURTHER THOUGHT OR DISCUSSION

1. What did your dad do well as a father? What did he do poorly?

2. If you are a dad, are there distinct ways in which you behave as a father that are different from what you experienced? What are they?

3. If you're not a biological dad, do you see yourself as a father figure, or spiritual father, to anyone? To whom? How did that relationship develop?

4. Is there a particular difficulty you experience in your relationship with your kids, or anyone with whom you have a "father" relationship? Who can you go to for advice on how to improve those relationships?

5. What is one area for growth you want to work on as a father or father figure?

CHAPTER

YOUR LEGACY TO CHILDREN

S everal years ago I had one of the most transformational realizations of my life. I was many years into my role with a missionary organization in which I led a staff whose responsibility was to prepare missionary candidates for two years of cross-cultural ministry overseas.

It was deeply rewarding but challenging work because a crucial part of our task was to identify those who had significant and unresolved emotional wounds from the past. We knew those wounds would invariably surface in the course of challenging ministry demands and would frequently result in conflict on teams as well as the unexpected early return of team members from their fields of service.

We were aided in this process by very capable professional therapists, some of whom had spent many years in cross-cultural ministry themselves. Through testing and personal interviews they helped us determine which candidates had issues that had to be resolved prior to going abroad. I had the unenviable job of informing heartbroken candidates that there were issues in their lives, unhealed wounds, that kept us from approving them for overseas assignments.

Over time I began to notice a recurring theme, which became a predictable pattern, which became a glaring spotlight pointing out the obvious. The pattern for those with very clear emotional or spiritual pain was almost always the same. It didn't matter if the candidate was a woman or a man, single or married. When the layers of their stories were peeled away the same character was virtually always in the center of their wounds—their fathers.

The outward issue may have been anger, poor self-esteem, inability to trust others, or a palpable fear in close-knit settings, but the father was in the center of the story. I subsequently learned with many candidates that when I saw the familiar patterns of deep woundedness coming to the surface with their teams I needed to ask them one question, "Can you tell me about you and your father?"

What was initially a shock became a source of conviction for me regarding my own fathering, and then an indictment on the horrific and increasing pattern of unhealthy fathers passing their own woundedness on to their children. This singularly influential experience is what caused me to leave two decades of cross-cultural ministry to start a ministry directed to men, and fathers in particular.

Fathers have the potential to be a source of profound emotional damage or profound blessing to their children. Nothing in a child's life has a deeper impact for harm or for good than the presence, touch, and voice of his or her father. Or his absence.

Malachi 4:6 says of God: "He will turn the hearts of the fathers to their children, and the hearts of the children to their fathers; or else I will come and strike their land with a curse" (NIV '84). This verse describes the crucial connection between fathers and children, and either blessing or a curse. When fathers' hearts are directed toward their children, their children respond likewise, and blessings occur. When fathers pull away and ignore their children, the children respond in kind, and curses ensue.

I can't think of another culture where the truth of this verse has been more sadly revealed than in the United States over the past 50 years. We have turned from a culture in which father figures were revered and respected to one in which fathers are portrayed as controlling, violent, or bumbling idiots. Their kids demean them and their wives carry all the meaningful authority in the household.

It's hard to believe that in the span of one generation males who observed TV father models in shows such as *Father Knows Best* and *Leave It To Beaver* now see the examples of *The Simpsons*, *Family Guy*, and *Modern Family*.

We are even hearing serious claims by some women that men are not needed in the household beyond the provision of their seed. In fact, we're better off without them!

Does fatherlessness have any affect? Of course it docs. Despite the claims of those who say fathers have become dispensable, research proves otherwise (National Fatherhood Initiative and National Center for Fathering). Children from fatherless homes (or uninvolved dads) are:

- 5 times more likely to commit suicide
- 44 times more likely to commit rape
- 9 times more likely to drop out of high school
- 10 times more likely to abuse chemical substances
- 20 times more likely to end up in prison

Deep in the hearts of most dads I know is a quiet but persistent voice saying, "The most important calling I have in life is to my wife and children." It's so quiet that at times the noise of daily life overwhelms it. But when we pay close enough attention to hear, our spirit nods in agreement.

We ask ourselves: "How can we become the kind of fathers we want to be?"

Where in Scripture do we find examples of what a good father looks like? There aren't many. Go ahead; try to come up with two real-life biblical fathers we can use as role models.

Jesus' father, Joseph, demonstrated stunning humility, faithfulness, and patience in the face of a confusing calling, apparent unfaithfulness on his wife's part, and a son called into a role beyond anything his father could anticipate or relate to. Some have written eloquently about

Joseph, surmising what his heart must have been like based on his actions. But painfully little is revealed to those of us who want to follow his example in dealing with the everyday challenges we encounter.

Jesus painted a powerful picture in his upside-down description of a godly father's deep commitment to forgiveness, humility, and unconditional love to his prodigal son (Luke 15:11–32). It's one of the best pictures of a father in all of Scripture and serves as a wonderful look into the heart of God the Father. But after all, even that father was a symbol, not a real-life character.

Much more frequently, particularly in the Old Testament, we see examples of broken relationships between fathers and their children: David and Absalom, Saul and Jonathan. It's even most prominent in the lineage from Abraham through Jacob's sons in which a pattern of deceit, lies, and betrayal are passed on from father to son to brother.

It seems we gain the most insight into fathering from small snippets of information in verses throughout Scripture. One such passage is 1 Thessalonians 2:11–12, where Paul gives a glimpse of good fathering as he describes his relationship to the church in Thessalonica. "For you know that we dealt with each of you as a father deals with his own children, encouraging, comforting and urging you to live lives worthy of God."

This is not an exhaustive treatment of the subject, but I like the breadth: A good father *encourages, comforts,* and *inspires.* What can we learn from this brief, but deep, description of fathering in these two verses?

WE CAN BECOME FATHERS
WHO *ENCOURAGE* OUR CHILDREN

Here are three practical ways we can encourage our kids:

1. Give our time. Nothing speaks to a child that she is valued more than the fact that her father is willing to spend time with her. Studies indicate that dads average three minutes a day of uninterrupted time with their children. That's not quite enough.

We dads struggle mightily with the challenges of fitting all our priorities into our 16 wakeful hours a day. How do we fit it all in?

Here's the answer: We don't. We simply must understand we can't fit it ALL in. Some things get left out. The key is to put the most important issues into our schedules first and work around them. Are our kids important to us? We prove it by giving them our time.

Perhaps you're familiar with the illustration in which a man has two large containers and two similarly sized piles of large rocks, two piles of pebbles, and two piles of sand. He is told to put all of one pile of sand, then pebbles, then rocks into one container. He begins with the sand, followed by the smaller pebbles, but when it comes to the large rocks, he can only get a few into the container; there isn't enough space to get them all in.

He is asked to repeat the process with the three remaining piles, which are exactly the same size, but to fill the container with the large rocks first. He does so, then puts in the pebbles, which fill the open spaces and nooks between the large rocks. Finally, he pours in the sand. Like the pebbles it seeps to the bottom, filling in space. He is able to get most of the sand in except for just a small pile.

The point is, when it comes to our time, put the big rocks in first. Decide what are truly our highest priorities in life. Provision, yes, but also marriage and family. Those big rocks need to go into our calendars and schedules before the smaller pebbles of other commitments, more time at work, and the sand of wasted time. In the end, more will get into the container of our time, and what doesn't will be sand anyway, not rocks.

The truth about our schedules is we can't fit everything in. Let's make sure that time with each of our children is one of the first big rocks we put into the time we have available.

We dads need to give our children our time.

2. Give our attention. Time invested with our children is the first step; it gets reinforced or diluted by whether we bring our attention with our time.

As my kids grew older I thought I became pretty good at watching TV or reading the paper while acting like I was listening to them describe their day at school or with friends. Until one asked, "Dad, are you listening to me?" My lack of attention silently responded, "No, I'm ignoring you. I'm actually watching TV."

A good father learns how to flip the switch from work to home. If you work outside the home, consider some geographical point on your way home where you will flip the switch from being consumed with work matters to paying attention to matters at home.

Perhaps it's when you turn off the lights in your workplace. Or when you pass a certain sign on the highway that lets you know your off-ramp is coming up.

If you don't work outside the home, make even more of an effort to have a mental switch you turn off. The easiness and temptation of going back to your home office, or doing email on the computer in the family room, means you'll have to draw an even stronger line between work, home, and family. You can figure out where the switch is and make a mental note to always flip it when the workday is done.

In-depth participation in our children's worlds means that we really listen when they speak. We drop the paper or the smartphone; we look them in the eye and ask for more information. This gives the message: "Your life is important to me. I value who you are."

We dads need to give our attention to our children.

3. *Give our affirmation.* What a dad tells his kids about themselves, they will believe the rest of their lives. A dad's words form the foundation of what kids will think about themselves. We need to be one of the strongest voices in our kids' lives that build them up, not tear them down.

Colossians 3:21 reminds us not to deflate our children's spirits. Instead, our words should lift them up and encourage them toward paths that are healthy and life-giving. We need to catch our kids doing things right rather than solely focusing on when we catch them screwing up. When we see them doing well we should speak words that affirm.

Does that mean we never correct or discipline? Of course not. One of our strongest roles is to provide guidance, direction, and discipline. But when we do, we should correct their behavior, never tear down their value and who they are.

We should make direct observations about an action they haven't completed or done well enough: "You didn't really finish cleaning your room." Not, "Why do you always have to be so sloppy?" When we correct our kids, we should do so with words that address behavior, not harsh words that attack character.

Whenever possible we should praise our children. Focus on praise; minimize criticism. Again, our kids will internalize and believe the words we, as the father, speak to them and about them. We want our kids to know that while their behavior may not be acceptable, they are always the objects of our unconditional love.

Here's a related key point: Praise character, not performance. This is extremely important. Avoid always implying that you're proud of them primarily based on their behavior; rather, say something along the lines of, "I admire this about you."

There were numerous times in my childhood when I appreciated hearing my dad say, "Pal, I'm proud of you for _____." The fact is I was happy that he was proud. But over time I realized that I also carried lingering resentment that my dad's praise usually followed some kind of public performance, whether in sports or at church. Over time his words began to sound more like, "Craig, you did well. Keep it up. I'm watching."

There's no way that his intention was to communicate that his pride for me was based on my performance, or how well I reflected on him. But to a performance-oriented boy finding his way in the world, that's the way it began to feel.

Sure, let your daughter or son know that you're cheering on their successes, but be sure to take the additional step to notice what character quality lies beneath the surface of the action you want to encourage: "I really appreciate your dependability in taking care of your household responsibilities." Or, "You know what I admire about you? Your consideration for the needs of other people. I wish I was more like that."

Praise character qualities rather than behavior. And use words like "I admire, I respect, I appreciate," more often than, "I'm proud of you for..." This communicates objective respect for who they are on their own, rather than behavior that reflects well on you.

We dads need to affirm our children.

A good father encourages his children by giving his time, his attention and his affirmation. Nothing will ever replace the power of our time and our words in the lives of our children. Every one of us can do that.

WE CAN BECOME FATHERS WHO *COMFORT* OUR CHILDREN

Here are three examples of how we can do this:

1. Express love. The powerful impact of the words, "I love you" cannot be over-emphasized. I once watched a 35-year-old man weep over his father's death. He heard his dad was suddenly dying and barely clinging to life. He rushed to the hospital, sat at the foot of his father's bed, holding his hand, praying for him to regain consciousness.

The hope that drove him was to hear his dad say, "Son, I love you," for the first time. He never did. The powerful impact of the words, "I love you" cannot be over-emphasized. Nor can the impact of their absence.

Some men are reluctant to say, "I love you" to their kids. It's usually for one of two reasons: 1.) Because their fathers never said those words to them. If that's the case, that reveals more about their fathers' sense of self-worth than their own. 2.) Because they feel hurt by, or disappointed in, their kids. If that's the case, that reveals more about them than about their children's worth.

No one *earns* unconditional love, but we all crave it! Romans 5:8 tells us that even while we were still in sin, God loved us. That unconditional love was true in Paul's day and it remains true today about each one of us. Our kids long for the same grace we long for from God. Love that's undeserved, undemanded, unconditional. What they see of that love from us will give them a glimpse of what God's love is like.

"I love you." Men, give those words to your kids even if you never heard them yourself; even if your kids don't seem very loveable. Nothing will ever replace them.

We comfort our kids when we express love.

2. Touch frequently. Those who study such matters say that a simple touch from another person communicates worth and value. They go on to say that we need 25 touches with another person daily to maintain a sense of emotional connectedness. I know, reading that makes some of you cringe! I wish I could reach out and give you a big hug.

Throughout the world and across time a handshake has communicated a sense of straight-forwardness and trust. An arm on the shoulder or pat on the back communicates, "I see you. I want to be with you. I like you." It doesn't take much, just a reach of the hand, but that simple act of touch communicates volumes, even to kids who pretend they don't want it.

Sure, as our children get older they want less and less touch from their dads—on the outside. On the inside, they still find a well-timed, sincere pat on the back or an arm around the shoulder a reassuring message of comfort and support.

Our sons don't want to be babied and our daughters don't want to feel threatened; we must never compromise those boundaries of respect and security. But a good dad also finds ways to maintain appropriate contact with his kids. For me, I discovered "stealth hugging." When I wanted to give some form of physical affection to my growing sons, I'd suddenly grab them and pull them to the ground, rolling around with exaggerated grunts and fake "punches."

With Alec and Conor, we ruined a couple of perfectly fine mattresses that served as landing pads. But I got in a bunch of hugs and even a few stray kisses. Somehow they didn't seem to mind.

When my daughter, Barclay, entered her young teens, she grew noticeably distant both physically and emotionally. I needed to be big enough not to take that personally and smart enough to give her space that said, "You're safe with me."

But every now and then I'd grab her and wrestle her to the ground, like I would the boys. She would try to keep a straight face but would eventually end up squealing with delight. It's virtually impossible to put on a smug, straight face when your dad is acting like a grown-up child with you.

Eventually the ice would crack and she too would reveal a smile that broke into a giggle. It's stealth hugging.

3. *Listen actively.* We men often have a challenge when we're in conversations. We think we are a step or two ahead of the game, already knowing what others are going to say, and working out perfectly formed responses that will leave them speechless. Mission accomplished!

Yeah, not really. The point of conversation, and even respectful and constructive arguments, is to engage with the other person. We need to hear, not only the words, but also the feelings behind the words. This is terrifically hard to do.

When our kids blow up in anger and say things like, "I can't stand you! I wish you weren't my dad!" it is unbelievably hard to deal with our own emotions let alone try to feel what's behind theirs.

One of my sons was misbehaving and through the course of our conversation we got into an argument. Eventually I lost my temper. I sent him to his room so both he and I could calm down.

A while later, when I went into his room to resume the conversation, he was lying on his bed strumming his guitar. He looked at me disdainfully and asked, "What are you doing in my room?"

Well, what I wanted to say was, "I just came in to throw you out the window." It took everything I had to hold my tongue and simply say, "I don't know" and walk away. Right then, the best I could do was not explode or strike out in anger. I had to get away.

Later I returned and began by apologizing for losing my temper with him. It led to a talk where I was able to genuinely feel his anger and frustration with me. And I was able to tell him mine with him. I still pretty much wanted to throw him out the window, but I managed to hold back.

Men, our kids are non-verbally saying, "Listen to me; feel what I feel." They are asking, "Is my heart safe with you? Or will you step on it?"

When they make some statements they are sending out trial balloons just to see what the relationship weather is like. We need to recognize those and think: How am I going to react? With more anger, punishment, preaching? Or will I respond with active listening that says, "I want to hear, I want to understand, and I want to feel what you feel. Your feelings are safe with me. But let's talk to each other respectfully."

A father comforts by expressing love, touching frequently, and listening actively.

WE CAN BECOME FATHERS WHO *INSPIRE* OUR CHILDREN

We can inspire our kids. There are several ways to do this:

1. Teach them biblical truth. Our parents may have done a much better job of practicing family devotions around the dinner table than we ever will. Mine sure did. My parents had regular dinner devotions and had us memorize Scripture. We knew the books of the Bible forwards and back and at one point were memorizing 12 verses a week, for which we got "tested" by a Sunday school teacher.

On one occasion, my father finished a Bible devotional and asked my sister and brothers for our comments. I chose that moment to finally release some pent-up gas, which reverberated off the hardwood chair and effectively shut down the spiritual tenor of this special family time. I thought I was hilarious. My dad thought I needed to spend the rest of the evening in my room.

Today's active, not to say frantic, pace of life often makes a communal dinner with everyone present a nearly unreachable goal. As kids get older and schedules get even more complicated the idea of family devotions becomes a lost cause. Not only that, our kids encounter thousands of electronic messages and video bits every day. How do we counter that with dry readings that even we cringed at 30 years earlier? If we had them at all?

One solution is to become more creative in our reading by using old "parables" that have been set in a new, modern context. J.R.R. Tolkien's *Lord of the Rings* books and movie series could hardly have been more popular. C.S. Lewis' Narnia stories have been retold in enthralling movies. Reading those books and watching the movies with an intentional periodic discussion about the meaning beneath the story is a great way to bring the gospel into our current culture. You and friends may know of many other options like these.

But men, here is a core point: our daily decisions, actions, and priorities speak far more clearly to our kids than words alone ever will. Teaching biblical truth is more a matter of consistent exposure to a belief system that truly affects our lives than about occasionally passing on Christian information.

Deuteronomy 6:1–9 indicates that we fathers instruct our kids by the full impact of words and behavior all the time: at home, away from home, at rest and at work. Everything we do and say, all the time, is some kind of testimony to our kids about what we believe.

They will learn far more about the reality of our faith by seeing how we treat those around us and what principles we base our decisions on than they ever will from devotions alone. We need to live it, not just preach it. In fact, if we preach it and don't live it, we can be sure they will eventually reject it.

We inspire our kids by teaching and modeling biblical truth to them.

2. *I'll explain this next point this way.* I have a friend with four grown sons, each of whom is a committed Christ-follower. My kids, all in their 30s, are the same. So far. Some time ago I said to him, "You know as well as I do there are no guarantees how our kids will turn out. And in some ways, we still don't know for sure. It's mostly through God's grace, and our kids' own choices. BUT…if there is one thing you'd encourage other dads to practice with their kids, what would that be?"

His answer was exactly what mine is: *model authenticity.*

One of the most important ways to inspire our kids to become Christ-followers is to be genuine, honest, real people, willing to reveal our vulnerabilities, our flaws, and fears. When we don't reveal our struggles and temptations, our kids think we don't have any.

The conclusion they can reach is: they shouldn't have any struggles or temptations either. Eventually they are going to find out the truth anyway; we all have plenty of flaws. If the model they have seen in us is, "Present the impressive, hide the bad," they will follow the same model until it no longer works, or they can no longer fake it. They'll wonder:

If Christianity is a faith of grace and forgiveness, why is it so important to try to fool people with who you are? If Dad never had any problems, why do I? If he did, why didn't he ever trust me with the truth?

German philosopher Friedrich Nietzsche wrote, "What was silent in the father speaks in the son, and I often found in the son the unveiled secret of the father" (*The Gay Science*). Whatever we may think about Nietzsche's view of life and God, I think he had this one right. Family secrets and generational sins that remain hidden and unhealed will reveal themselves in the next generation.

I'm revealing a very personal lesson here, men. As I've mentioned earlier, this is my story. I had a wonderfully Christ-like dad who was impressive in many ways. I literally never heard him swear or saw him get angry. I never heard from him that he struggled with any temptation, never knew where he was vulnerable. His example was in many ways an enormous gift. It was also a heavy yoke to carry.

I could have used a story or two from him where he started by saying, "Craig, this is hard for me to reveal, but I want you to know this about me and my journey..."

Revealing our own story with our kids is deeply important. Of course, we don't reveal inappropriate details before a child is emotionally prepared to handle them. Nor do we tell stories that have no redemptive value. But those cautions are no excuse to take family secrets to the grave.

My advice, dads, is to tell the right story to the right child at the right time.

When my second son, Conor, was 11, Beryl and I noticed his behavior changing. He seemed more sullen (it's when the throw-you-out-the-window incident happened), he was uncharacteristically struggling in school, and we suspected he was lying to us.

One day Beryl came to me with our phone bill, which had a few 900 number charges. That prefix indicated a sex-talk phone number. She confronted me with it, "Do you know anything about this?"

My first reaction was relief. No, I had no idea where it came from. It wasn't me. In the next instant my heart sank. One of the boys does know something about it. I was afraid it was Conor.

I didn't know how to conduct this unexpected conversation for which I'd had no training. So I did the most logical thing, I took him to 31 Flavors. Ice cream always helps tough love go down. But I still had no idea what to say or where to start.

So I started with my story. I told Conor my experience of rejection by my best friends in junior high, an experience that caused me to pull into myself. I told him of a pattern of lying to cover up I'd developed ever since I was a boy. I told him of my first exposure to pornography.

When I did, to my deep gratitude, Conor opened up. It turned out he was experiencing almost exactly the same things every day; we just didn't know it. A close friend had rejected him and was trying to convince others to do the same. His loneliness at school was affecting his ability to focus on his studies and another friend talked him into dialing a 900 number while at our house. My story was being retold in my son and I didn't know it. We had a profound conversation and were able to clear the air on a number of things.

Afterward he turned to me and said simply, "Dad, I'm glad we got this off our chests."

Yeah, me too.

Men, our children's honesty begins with our own honesty. Their secrets begin with ours.

"What was silent in the father speaks in the son…"

I just about wept when I read that for the first time, and knew its truth. Please, I urge you, do not keep your story hidden from your children. At the right age, tell the right story to the right child. You'll know when it's right. And it's sooner than you think.

Model authenticity.

3. *Discipline consistently and grace-fully.* Proverbs 19:18 makes it pretty clear; in discipline there is hope and a lack of discipline brings death. A good father courageously enters into circumstances that are frequently filled with complexity and uncertainty. He refuses to remain passive; he corrects sinful or hurtful behavior on the part of his children.

A good father also recognizes the brokenness of his own heart. Sometimes our demands of our children are more for our "image" than for our kids' benefit. A courageously honest dad faces his own brokenness, explores his own motives, discerns what issues are paramount, and then stands his ground. His discipline is full of grace—and fully aware of his own woundedness.

Have you ever asked yourself: What is behind my frustration or anger? It's a crucial question if we want to discipline our children with grace rather than just reaction. We need to ask: Is this matter more about protecting my image or protecting my child's heart? Our response may reveal more about us than it does about our children.

When we feel angry about some behavior on our child's part, the underlying emotion is almost always fear. And for men, the deepest fear is always: What if I lose the respect of others?

There is such a thing as righteous anger. The Bible says, "In your anger do not sin" (Ephesians 4:26). Righteous anger is always in defense of a worthwhile principle or about someone else's safety or respect. That type of anger is righteous. It's the anger Jesus showed in the temple, for example, when he tossed the tables of the money-changers. It's the anger he showed most frequently toward the hypocritically pious religious leaders who condemned others' sin.

Sinful anger is the opposite. It's never on behalf of others; it's always about self-advancement, self-exaltation, self-promotion. Jesus' anger was never about his own image or reputation. Nor should ours be.

We also need to pick the hills we are willing to die on. We need to be intentionally selective in the issues that we decide are valuable enough for us to go to DEFCON 3. In other words, "I'm willing to fight over this one."

Some issues are absolutely worth the effort, tension, and conflict that arises when a family value is at risk or is being ignored. In my opinion, there are relatively few of these, but here are some examples:

- If you speak disrespectfully to Mom, we're going to have a serious conversation.
- Son, you call your sister a demeaning name, I'll let you know how strongly I feel about that.

- You cheat in school, that's a problem.
- You embrace our culture's values of morality and faith, I'm going to engage you directly about my concerns about that.
- You dye your hair orange, and it's hanging in your eyes...not sure I want to die on that hill. I'm going to let that one go because my main reaction is about me—I feel embarrassed because of what others might think of me as a dad or man. It's not the choice I would prefer you make, but it has nothing to do with morality or respect toward others. It just makes you look weird. This too shall pass.

Disciplining grace-fully also includes knowing when and how to apologize. It is powerful when a person in authority has the guts and integrity to say, "I'm sorry. I was wrong." Willingly do so whenever it's true.

And don't ever give anything but a full, complete apology. Today we see ridiculous public statements that are supposed to pass as apologies: "If my actions were offensive to some I regret that they were construed that way." That is deflecting blame, not accepting it.

My wife gave me some helpful advice by pointing out, "If your apology has a 'but' in it, don't even bother." She's absolutely right. If we say we're sorry about some action or word, and then follow it immediately with the word "but," we are making an excuse for whatever we just apologized for. Don't bother. Keep your buts out of it.

When we apologize we take ownership. A sincere apology has the potential to profoundly deepen a relationship. It is a window for redemption. It transforms an action that wounds into an action that heals.

4. Cast a vision. An engaged dad pays close attention to who his daughter is, what she loves, how she is gifted, and what she has to offer others. He resists the temptation to push her into the most prestigious school, or lucrative career, simply for the sake of family reputation.

Men, pay attention to your son's God-given skills, gifts, and values. Reflect them back to him every time you spot them. "Son, did you know that you have a great ear for music?" "Hey, pal, you have unusual wisdom for a boy your age."

Watch your children to see what they love and are gifted in, and regularly point it out to them.

Proverbs 22:6 says, "Raise up a child in the way he should go, and when he is old he will not depart from it." Clearly that means that we teach our children right and wrong. With God's grace and with their own choices they will return to those convictions even if for a while they cast them aside.

But the truth is, sometimes they won't. How else can we honestly recognize that some children never return? And some parents have to watch in horror as their children live a destructive life, never to return. I can't imagine the agony.

I believe this verse also means we should watch to see who God has made our sons and daughters to be, and then encourage them in that direction. When they get older they will follow it freely, joyfully, and fruitfully.

We should avoid the temptation to push them toward our preferred future: carry on the family business, get a prestigious job, or make up for regrets we have in life. These will only cause future turmoil and resentment on their part.

If *they* make these choices, great! Our kids are God's creation, not ours. We should honor who they are as a sacred part of God's creativity. They may be, at heart, extremely different from us. Our job is to help them identify God's calling for their lives, not ours. And if we do that well, they will gladly embrace those gifts, passion, and calling the rest of their lives.

Finally, we inspire our children when we...

5. *Give them our blessing.* I know a man who has struggled with self-esteem all his life. He lacks confidence, he is fearful, he has never fully used his gifts and abilities. Eventually I found out that when he was young his dad constantly demeaned him with comments like, "You'll never amount to anything. You're nothing but a failure. I'm ashamed of you."

Those words speak death to a child. Those words fashion a lifestyle and become part of a destructive legacy. They should *never* pass the lips of a father.

The first words spoken by the heavenly Father recorded in the New Testament appear in Matthew 3:17. Following Jesus' baptism, the heavens opened and God spoke:

"This is my Son, whom I love; with him I am well pleased."

Every son and daughter needs to hear words like that from his or her father, words spoken in public that demonstrate belonging, worth, and fatherly pride. What a difference between those words and the words of shame and condemnation mentioned above! Enormous, life-altering difference!

Do you know the words God spoke of his Son are his words about you? They are, because you are completely forgiven. Through the washing of Jesus' innocent blood, when God sees those of us who have accepted that gift of grace, he sees justification, he sees forgiveness. The work is done on the cross. Done.

God sees you and says, "I am thrilled with Tom!" "I am so proud of Bill!" "I love Mike! He's my son, and I am well pleased with him." Those are God's words over you!

Have you said those words to your son or daughter? This is one of a dad's most powerful legacies: speaking blessing and affirmation to his kids.

One of the most important truths I know of for fathers is this: Boys learn masculinity from their dads. Dad is the model. The son's sense of significance and identity as a young man is also affirmed by his dad.

Girls, of course, learn femininity from Mom. She's the model. But the daughter's sense of significance and identity as a young woman is confirmed by her dad.

Dads bestow the value of masculinity and femininity to their sons and daughters. They convey innate worth through their words. A father's voice represents God's voice to every son and daughter. The voice of the father communicates value and worth, or it communicates shame and rejection.

Dads, this is one of the most profound callings in your role with your children, yet the world will deny it. Those who do are wrong.

It's about the father. When a father withholds blessing from his son, the son will look for it in a community of men through performance or destruction. Or else he will retreat into defeat and passivity.

When a father withholds blessing from his daughter, she will look for it in the words and the arms of another man. It doesn't necessarily matter who the man is; he just needs to be a male. Some of the women reading this already know this from personal experience.

Mothers bring deep impact into the lives of their children; and they seem to intuitively understand this. They sacrificially give their lives to bring love, safety, provision, and presence into the lives of their kids.

It's dads who so often seem to confuse their value and their role. Fathers are called to speak words of blessing into the lives of others, whether to their wives, their children, or other men.

Some of you are stepfathers. If you already fully embrace your role with your stepchildren as if they are your own flesh and blood, good for you. Your words still carry the weight of a father. Their biological father may have abdicated his role in your stepchildren's lives, but they should never be condemned to pay the price for his irresponsibility. YOU can be the voice of the father in their lives.

Just like God the Father did with Jesus, every good father finds the time and place to say about his child, "Hey, everyone! This is my daughter. I love her and I am deeply proud of who she is. Just wanted to let you know."

This simple passage, 1 Thessalonians 2:11–12, gives a wonderful description of the impact of good dads: "We dealt with you as a father deals with his own children, encouraging, comforting and urging you to live lives worthy of the glory of God."

Dads, our gift to our kids is to bring encouragement, comfort, and inspiration into their lives. To guide them into an understanding of all God created them to be.

The role of a father is not an easy one. It is enormously challenging. It is one of the two most significant roles of our lives if we are married and have children. In most cases, we had very little training before-hand; and the primary model we had was flawed. But there is no calling more profound or rewarding. It is the role most often referred to in the New Testament about God himself: Father.

None of us dads are everything we want to be. None of us will ever be perfect dads, but with intention and commitment we can all be good enough dads.

Men, we have a powerful, life-giving impact on our children; and through them, we impact the future. That's the legacy of a father. There is no more important legacy we can possibly leave behind.

QUESTIONS
FOR FURTHER THOUGHT OR DISCUSSION

1. What did your dad do well as a father? What did he do poorly?

2. If you are a dad, are there distinct ways in which you behave as a father that are different from what you experienced? What are they?

3. If you're not a biological dad, do you see yourself as a father figure, or spiritual father, to anyone? To whom? How did that relationship develop?

4. Is there a particular difficulty you experience in your relationship with your kids, or anyone with whom you have a "father" relationship? Who can you go to for advice on how to improve those relationships?

5. What is one area for growth you want to work on as a father or father figure?

CHAPTER

YOUR LEGACY
TO THE WORLD

As mentioned in Chapter 1, one of the best-known quotes about the state of men is Henry David Thoreau's, "The mass of men live lives of quiet desperation…" Even though he wrote those words more than 150 years ago, they still hold true for many men. We men, and the women who know us well, are familiar with the silent pressure, the hidden doubt, and the unmet longings we often encounter in life.

As familiar as Thoreau's quote is, the shocking truth is that the second half of it is virtually unknown, "The mass of men live lives of quiet desperation… and die with their song still in them." (There is some question as to whether this second half originated with Thoreau. Until proven otherwise, I'm giving him credit.)

I find those last eight words stunning. They imply something I firmly believe—there is a "song" in every man. Through God's grace and sovereignty he has placed unique giftedness, talent, and conviction into the heart of every man. It's his song! But as Thoreau noticed, most men go to the grave without singing it.

Sadly, the song sung by most men goes more like this:

Joy at the start
Fear in the journey
Joy in the coming home
A part of the heart
Gets lost in the learning
Somewhere along the road

Along the road
Your path may wander
A pilgrim's faith may fail
Absence makes the heart grow stronger
Darkness obscures the trail

Cursing the quest
Courting disaster
Measureless nights forebode
Moments of rest
Glimpses of laughter
Are treasured along the road

Joy at the start
Fear in the journey
Joy in the coming home
A part of the heart
Gets lost in the learning
Somewhere along the road.

Dan Fogelberg wrote these haunting lyrics to *Along the Road.* They are the current soundtrack for many men. Initially there may be joy in our life journey but something gets lost on the way. What gets lost? It's openness, boundlessness, joy, even passion.

What do we mean by "passion?" When we hear that word our minds go immediately to excitement, emotion, or sexual desire. These are legitimate examples of passion, but there is more to it. Passion is an intense enthusiasm for something. It's a conviction, a belief, or a set of circumstances that compel us to action.

Somewhere along the road many men lose a sense of passion—or realize they never had it in the first place.

My mom used to tell me that when I was a boy I always seemed to have a smile on my face. I apparently was a happy-go-lucky little guy, much more aware of the joys in life than the disappointments. I had a bizarre habit of wearing a circular, rubber tire tread taken from a toy bulldozer on my head, as some sort of crown I guess. I was showing the world I had no worries—certainly no concerns about their opinions of my taste in fashion.

Fast forward to 1989. I was 36 and a different person. Dan Fogelberg's insightful lyrics felt like the theme song to my life. In the words of another poet/writer, Parker Palmer, "I had found a noble way of living a life that was not my own, a life spent imitating heroes instead of listening to my own heart" (*Let Your Life Speak: Listening for the Voice of Vocation*).

That phrase described me at the time; it may describe some of you today. I had a wonderful job with an outstanding mission agency. I believed deeply in cross-cultural service and outreach. I had significant responsibilities for the oversight of the candidate-training program, their priorities on the field, and their pastoral care. I enjoyed the camaraderie and respect of my colleagues. But those who knew me would not have called me happy-go-lucky, let alone passionate about my work.

Probably they'd call me committed, perhaps dedicated, maybe even gifted...just not passionate.

Others *were* passionate about missions. They would go on about "contextualization" and the "homogeneous unit principle." They knew about the cause and effect of missionary casualties and "fishing" where the fish were biting. Clearly, people needed to be talking about these important matters. I just wasn't one of them.

I joined in on the fringes of the conversations—for 15 years. I managed to be better than competent, but I was hardly passionate.

Rather, I was discouraged and disappointed with the direction of my life. I was putting in time at a good ministry, performing on a B+/A-level. By all appearances I was at the pinnacle of my career. Most who knew me figured I was a lifer at that ministry.

But those few who knew me well might have noticed that I was losing my heart. I was stuck in a noble way of living that was not my own. What had happened to that open, trusting, happy-go-lucky boy my mom described? Somewhere along the road I had lost my passion.

Thank God, I eventually found it again.

Glory and Passion

In early 1990 Beryl and I saw a movie that changed my life. It was an encounter with passion. *Glory* is the true story of the Massachusetts 54th regiment in the Civil War. Except for a handful of white officers, the 54th was made up of recently freed slaves. Their hope was to serve with pride and to fight for the cause of their freedom.

They discovered, however, that they were simply intended to perform menial labor for the white troops. They were given the most demeaning tasks; they were beaten and whipped mercilessly for any infraction. This was not at all the opportunity to fight for their freedom that drew them to enlist.

Then they had their chance for glory. They volunteered to lead the charge on Fort Wagner on the South Carolina coast. It was virtually impregnable. Because it was so well designed, only one regiment at a time could attack. And it had to be from the front, right into the teeth of rifle and cannon fire.

Such an attack would mean certain death for most of the troops, but they would provide the crucial piercing maneuver for those who would follow. The black troops lined up along the coast with the fort on the horizon. They marched forward, and then raced toward the fort, taking enormous casualties from mortars, canons, and rifle fire. It was an incredible demonstration of character and bravery.

As the movie ended I felt a volcano of emotions welling up inside me. Tears streamed down my cheeks. Beryl and I left the theater and sat in the car in silence, my hands, white-knuckled, on the steering wheel. And then I wept. Uncontrollably. I convulsed with deep visceral sobs for several minutes, tears and snot covering my face. Once I regained my composure, Beryl, with concern and bewilderment on her face, asked a very reasonable question: "What did that movie do to you?"

I didn't think through my response; it came directly from the gut: "I want to believe in something that much! I want to believe in something so deeply that I would walk into the teeth of fear for it! I want to believe in something so deeply that I would die for it!"

So do you. I believe an important part of our journey as men is to discover what that "something" is. We need to ask ourselves: What do we want to live for? What are we willing to die for? What do we feel passionate about? Identifying our source of passion, calling, or mission is one of the most crucial factors in living a joy-filled, meaning-filled life.

All of us have passion deep inside. Every now and then it rises to the surface when we:

- Go nuts cheering for a sports team
- Feel deep pleasure watching a sunset over a lake
- Marvel over an inspiring work of art or piece of music
- See a child being mistreated, and know there's nothing or no one who could stop you from protecting her

That's passion rearing its head.

John Eldredge says: "The deadened soul requires a greater and greater level of stimulation to arouse it" (*Journey of Desire*). As exciting as sports can be, there's something sadly unfulfilled or limited in a man whose greatest thrill in life is wearing the logo of a team whose players he will never know.

(I make no claim to being invulnerable to the joy of sports. Not long ago I traveled a thousand miles to view the Chicago Cubs in the World Series. I even watched the final victorious game 7 with my sons in a sports bar just south of Wrigley Field though the Cubs were playing in Cleveland. It will forever stand as a red-letter day in my life.)

The fan's primary growth in passion is to yell louder, become more rabid, buy more memorabilia, or transfer his allegiance to a more successful team. Is there something more?

Yes.

WHAT MEN DO

When men meet one another for the first time, you know what questions will arise: "What's your name? Where do you live? What do you do for a living?" Questions that probably won't arise are: "What are your roles in life? What is your story?" In our culture what men *do* apparently matters more than who men *are*.

Our society teaches us that work, wealth, and worldly success define our significance. We Christ-followers may agree that's a lie, in our heads, but the way we live reveals that, in our hearts, we tend to agree. Work defines our significance.

For many men, the word "work" brings to mind two F-words (well, for some there may be a third, but I'll stick with the first two):

Fulfillment: There is dignity in work itself because God designed, ordained, and granted it. He gave the very first man and woman work to do as a blessing. It was meant to provide a sense of contribution, authority, and impact (Genesis 1:28; 2:15, 19, 20). Whatever kind of legitimate work we do, it has an innate dignity and sacredness because God ordained it.

He created us, men in particular, with a deep longing to find fulfillment in the work we do. We want to matter. We want to know that we make a difference in the world. We want to have an impact.

Futility: God blessed humankind with work, but then everything changed—for the worse. Because of their sin in the Garden, God delivered soul-deep consequences that profoundly impacted Adam and Eve, and all men and women who have followed them. These consequences are not the same for men and women because the deepest heart longing of each is different.

Most women have a profound longing to give birth to new life. That incredible hope was cursed. "To the woman he said, 'I will make your pains in childbearing very severe; with painful labor you will give birth to children. Your desire will be for your husband, and he will rule over you'" (Genesis 3:16).

Men, the women you know have this going against them: the deep joy of birthing new life will cause them deep agony. In addition, they will long for acceptance from men. They will believe men's opinions of them determine their significance and value. In this way men will have power over them. Innumerable self-centered men have learned this foundational truth about women and taken advantage of it. It's a curse.

Similarly, a heartfelt longing for men suffered its own specific curse, one that pierces to a man's very core: work.

Cursed is the ground because of you;
through painful toil you will eat food from it all the days of your life.
It will produce thorns and thistles for you, and you will eat the plants of the field.
By the sweat of your brow you will eat your food
until you return to the ground, since from it you were taken;
for dust you are and to dust you will return. (Genesis 3:17–19)

The very gift that God gave men—work itself—was cursed. Until the day we die it will cause us to sweat and toil painfully. Along the way it will produce thorns and thistles. This stunning turnabout results in a love-hate tension almost all men have toward work. The very thing we long for, a sense of significance and meaning, brings hardship, agony, and decay.

We wonder why, if what we long for is accomplishment, impact, and significance, that our work so often leaves us feeling empty. It's because we think we are in control when we aren't. We think we have authority when we don't.

In his book, *From Wild Man to Wise Man*, Richard Rohr says so insightfully: "...on the job most men do not have much power...Most men are paid for doing what someone else wants done. They do not really control their own lives. No wonder so many men have become passive, and no wonder so many men seem angry."

Sound familiar? Work was given as a blessing but it's been cursed. It brings men both fulfillment and futility. As a result, we must guard our hearts and souls from the moral, and morale, challenges many jobs produce on a daily basis.

Now for the good news. Work is just that—work. It's for provision. It provides for our basic needs: housing, food, health, and warmth. For some it also provides significance, but for all it is cursed. It's an *occupation*. It occupies time and place.

Our word "occupation" comes from the Latin *occupatio*, which means "to take hold, to make one's own." In English that word refers to a person's means of making a living. It's about provision for ourselves and those who depend on us.

Our word "vocation," on the other hand, comes from the Latin *vocare*, which means "to call." Vocation is a summons or strong desire to pursue a certain calling. It's not necessarily about provision, it's about passion. It's what we love, what we are called to do. Fredrick Buechner says our calling is "the place where your deep gladness meets the world's deep need" (*Wishful Thinking: A Theological ABC*).

In response, Parker Palmer writes:

Buechner's definition starts with the self and moves toward the needs of the world: it begins, wisely, where vocation begins—not in what the world needs (which is everything), but in the nature of the human self, in what brings the self joy, the deep joy of knowing that we are here on earth to be the gifts that God created.

Vocation does not mean a goal that I pursue. It means a calling that I hear. Before I can tell my life what I want to do with it, I must listen to my life telling me who I am. I must listen for the truths and values at the heart of my own identity, not the standards by which I *must* live—but the standards by which I cannot help but live. (*Let Your Life Speak: Listening for the Voice of Vocation*)

For his early adult life, Jesus had an occupation as a carpenter. But immediately following the baptism of a prophet and the anointing of his Father, he focused on his vocation, his calling, which he described in different ways: To serve, not to be served (Mark 10:45); to preach Good News to the poor (Luke 4:18–19); to seek and save the lost (Luke 19:10); to give humanity life to the fullest (John 10:10).

I believe each of us also has a personal calling or mission that God has uniquely designed us for. Do you know what yours is? If not, the rest of this chapter will help you to discover it.

FINDING YOUR NORTH STAR

The North Star is one of the most significant stars in our galaxy, but when we look at the millions of stars in the night sky, it isn't immediately obvious. It doesn't blaze itself into prominence. You have to know where to look.

There are two unique aspects of the North Star: 1.) It is always visible. No matter where you travel in the northern hemisphere, you can see it. 2.) When you look at time-lapse photography of our galaxy, the stars all blur into curved dashes, circling around the sky. All except the North Star. It doesn't blur; it remains a steady light. All the other stars rotate around it.

The same is true for your mission; it is always visible no matter where you are. Once you find it, everything else rotates around it. It's your North Star and it's your legacy to the world.

At some point every man wants to know: Why am I here? Is there a point to my existence? What is my purpose? As we get older these kinds of questions multiply, especially if our current life focus has little purpose.

Some call this a midlife crisis. I call it a midlife awakening.

I also notice that these questions are not just being asked by men in their 40s and 50s, but by men in their upper 20s and early 30s. This younger generation is asking questions of significance at a much earlier age than my own. That's a good thing. Men feel a tug in our hearts that tells us to search for our calling and find our mission in life.

This is one of the core components to a man's journey. But sometimes we mistakenly think that until we find that one overriding, unique purpose, we are wasting our lives. The truth is subtler than that. We do have a unique calling from God, but there are elements to our mission that are deeper than that.

MISSION POSSIBLE

In his insightful book, *How to Find Your Mission in Life*, Richard Bolles makes a very astute observation. Those of us who are committed Christ-followers actually share two missions with each other, even before we identify our own mission. I describe these three missions—two common, one unique—in this way:

Mission One: To have an increasing awareness of God's presence in every moment of our lives.

Before investing time and energy into finding our North Star it's worth remembering our first and foremost calling is to know God and to enjoy him forever.

How well are we doing this?

If you're like me, you may spend time very focused on God's presence in your personal devotional time. You may be aware of God's presence as you pray over a meal, or attend church. But are we mindful of God in the mundane or even aggravating moments of the day?

- Is God's spirit present around the breakfast or dinner table?
- Am I aware of God's presence as the sun rises over the horizon in the morning?
- Do I see God's sovereignty even when my day starts to unravel?
- How well am I able to embrace the unplanned activities that insert themselves into my schedule?

Deuteronomy 4:39 tells us: "Acknowledge and take to heart this day that the LORD is God in heaven above and on the earth below. There is no other." When God feels close, or when he feels distant, our first calling is to become increasingly aware of his presence with us moment by moment. That's a mission we all share as Christ-followers.

Mission Two: To bring the presence of Christ with me into every encounter I have every day.

Do you have any idea how often I think primarily of my own benefit and not that of others? Of course you do, even though you don't know me, because you're pretty much the same as me.

I recall the guy I cut off changing lanes the other day. Hmmm, how well did I make his world a better place? Or I remember the woman behind the counter at Panera one wintry morning who seemed in a miserable mood. I asked how she was doing. Her response: She had gotten up at 3 a.m., left her son with her mother in Denver (an hour north) to make the drive in the snow to be there at 5 a.m. Just to serve me a bagel and coffee.

"OK, so other than that, how's your day going?"

There are ways we can make this world a better place for others each day.

- Kiss your wife in the morning; kiss your son
- Tell the Starbucks barista to keep the change; pay the extra dollar he forgot to charge you
- Give your neighbor a Christmas gift; shovel her driveway
- Toss a little extra into the Salvation Army bucket; ring the bell yourself next time
- Thank the admin assistant for the print job he did; shock him by doing the job for him next time
- Provide a meal for an orphan in Bolivia; do the same for a homeless man downtown
- Set up chairs at church; sweep the floor at home

Each one of these is doable and each one communicates to someone, "I care about you. Your life matters to me."

In doing so we bring the spirit of Jesus into someone else's day. That's the second mission we share.

Mission Three: To find and follow your own North Star. You do this by examining your life, your experience, and your aspirations in order to identify that sense of passion, calling, and mission you long for.

Your North Star has three components:

1. To use your greatest God-given *Talent*

2. For the benefit of the *People* who you care about
3. To bring about a *Principle* you believe in deeply

How do you find these components? First, think through, ask others, and ask God to show you what *Talent* you always bring to situations. It is an ability you've always had. You didn't go to school to learn it. It hasn't been trained into you. You may have worked to excel at it but it is unique in that God put it in you at birth.

The Talent that God put into you from the start is what you always bring to the table, and it isn't going away.

What is it?

You organize with clarity
You speak with insight
You build with energy
You design systems with efficiency
You counsel with wisdom
You teach with enthusiasm
You lead with courage
You serve with compassion
You defend with loyalty
You write with wit and insight

The list is virtually endless. There's a God-given Talent in you. It's what you love to do; it's what you do with amazing skill; and it's something the world needs more of.

Secondly, think through, ask others, and ask God to show you who are the *People* you care about in a unique way. Of course you care about your family; you *have* to love them. They're not the people I'm talking about.

There is a certain group of people who always seem to stand out to you. You notice them when you're driving, watching TV, praying, viewing a movie, and your heart goes out to them. Being a guy, you may not weep for them or emotionally gush about them every time they catch your attention. Or maybe you do.

Who are they?

Homeless people
Gulf war vets
Stressed-out businessmen
High school students
Young adults just starting their careers
Single mothers
Victims of sexual abuse
Those who are wandering spiritually
Political refugees
Depressed teenagers

This list is endless, too, but there's someone on it for you. There are certain People who stand out to you in a unique way. They aren't going away; they need you.

Thirdly, think through, ask others, and ask God to show you the *Principle* you believe in most deeply. You might ask, what's a principle? The Oxford dictionary says it's a basic underlying belief. I find that definition is OK but not good enough. A principle is a deep conviction that compels you. It's something you could see working for, living for, perhaps even dying for. Principles often inspire the most profound acts of courage and self-sacrifice.

Do you know what that Principle is for you?

Providing security or safety
Bringing understanding
Guiding someone into intimacy with God
Striving for excellence
Fighting for justice
Passing on wisdom
Providing comfort to those who struggle
Bringing health into someone's life
Demonstrating dignity to those who are ignored
Showing love to others

Like the other lists, this one is endless. Like the others, there is some-thing here specifically for you. There is something that drives you and it isn't going away. How do I know? Because it's what I believe about how God operates. He uses us to accomplish his purposes. And it's what I be-lieve about men—you matter. You have something to bring to the world. Men touch people and those people change, for better or for worse.

Here's one more very important clue: What suffering have you ex-perienced in life? There is often a direct correlation between *pain* and *passion*. The core meaning of the word "passion" is "suffering."

For countless people there is a link between pain we experience and a resulting deep conviction to do something to relieve that kind of pain in others.

After 9/11 thousands of Americans signed up for military service. Nothing was going to stop them from putting their lives on the line to ensure the security of the U.S.

After losing a daughter to a drunk driver in 1980 Candy Lightner started Mothers Against Drunk Drivers (MADD). Nothing was going to stop her.

After losing his son to an abductor in 1981 John Walsh, a hotel man-agement executive, started the TV show *America's Most Wanted.* Their web-site says, "John Walsh has turned his passion for justice into the nation's number one crime-fighting show." Nothing was going to stop him.

After wrestling for years with questions about my significance and wondering whether I had what it takes to be a man—whatever that meant—I felt compelled to help other men with their own journeys because I'm convinced they matter.

Frequently, not always, but frequently, our greater life-long purpose, our North Star, is defined by suffering we have experienced or been exposed to, and a conviction we develop to prevent or relieve that pain in others.

LIVING ON PURPOSE

So where do we go from here? We ask God's guidance in composing a life-purpose mission statement that inspires and reminds us of our North Star.

Following are ideas to prompt your thinking. I encourage you to meditate, pray, and ask others who know you well to help you identify the Talent and People and Principle that God has placed in you. Here's a partial list of Talents people have, expressed as verbs, People groups that may stand out, and Principles men and women believe in deeply. Yours may be on these lists, or not. This is just to get you started.

Verbs that demonstrate *Talents*:

Launch, Empower, Challenge, Inspire, Encourage, Model, Demonstrate, Organize, Order, Clarify, Produce, Simplify, Increase, Defend, Expand, Protect, Discover, Inspire, Serve, Teach, Support, Build, Perfect, Release, Liberate, Promote, Communicate, Write, Connect, Strengthen, Create, Sing, Equip, Unify, Train, Repair, Guide, Lead, Convince, Paint

People who stand out:

Poor, Sick, Families, Leaders, Children, Athletes, Men, Women, Christians, Orphans, Oppressed, Needy, Parents, Homeless, Students, Business people, Hungry, Refugees, Imprisoned, Widows, Singles, Confused, Desperate, Endangered, Wealthy, Successful, Teens, Spiritually Lost, Hopeless, Rejected, Unpopular, Strangers, Internationals, Unemployed, Frightened, Neighbors, Defenseless, Teachers

Principles that are deeply important:

Freedom, Excellence, Hope, Integrity, Dreams, Passion, Healing, Truth, Compassion, Dignity, Value, Self Esteem, Harmony, Purpose, Order, Beauty, Honor, Nobility, Loyalty, Service, Meaning, Love, Strength, Justice, Faithfulness, Intimacy, Courage, Respect, Life, Joy, Honesty, Humility, Wisdom, Kindness, Salvation, Protection, Comfort, Victory, Health, Worship, Generosity, Perseverance

Finally, consider whether there is some pain or suffering you've experienced that brings passion to the surface. It may well be that your North Star has something to do with relieving or preventing that kind of pain in others.

Once you've identified one or two words in each category that are true for you, try putting them into a mission statement. My approach to mission statements is that at a certain point more becomes less. More words actually muddle and confuse what compels us.

To help overcome the tendency to say too much, use this approach: Include every word that absolutely *must* be included, but ruthlessly eliminate every word that is unnecessary or "fluff." Fluff would be words or phrases that can be assumed, such as, "To the best of my abilities…" or "Because I want to change the world, I…"

Sometimes fluff has a spiritual layer that blurs the language rather than sharpens it: "So that my life might be honoring to God, I…" or "As God grants me strength, I…" These phrases go without saying, so don't say them. Keep your North Star mission statement clear, concise, and memorable.

Use the following template for crafting your mission statement:

My mission is to __Talent/Verb__ for __People__ so they can experience __Principle__.

OR,

I am compelled to provide __Principle__ by __Talent/Verb__ for __People__.

The specific order isn't important; what is important is making it inspiring and memorable for you.

Jesus described his mission this way: I have come to seek and to save those who are lost. (Talent/Verb: He came [incarnation]. Principle: Salvation. People: Those who are lost.)

My North Star: I guide and inspire men on their life journey, to help them pass on a life-giving legacy. (Talent/Verb: Guide, inspire. People: Men. Principle: Life-giving legacy.)

My wife's North Star: I create beauty to reflect the glory of God's creation to the world (Talent/Verb: Create beauty. People: The world. Principle: Reflect the glory of God's creation.)

Another example: I demonstrate compassion to those who grieve, so they can feel the Father's love. (Talent/Verb: Demonstrate compassion. People: Those who grieve. Principle: Love.)

What is your mission statement?

When and where can you put this into practice? In your home? In your church? In your community? At work? Start thinking about ways you can pursue this passion on a regular basis regardless of your occupation. Perhaps you commit one afternoon or evening a week to your North Star. Perhaps you commit one day a month, or one week a year to bringing hope to others whose life circumstances compel you to work on their behalf.

I'll remind you again, there is dignity in your work, your occupation, your source of provision. And there is inspiration in your calling, your vocation, your source of passion. It just might be that as you engage more fully in living out your North Star, these two arenas—provision and passion, occupation and vocation—will merge and become one and the same.

That's what happened for me. Shortly after watching *Glory* I committed to discovering what my true North Star was. Not long afterward, I was having lunch with a good friend who was on staff at a church that Beryl and I longed to be a part of someday. He asked me, "Craig, would you be open to interviewing for a staff position at Willow Creek?"

"Are you kidding!" I replied. "Yes. What kind of position?"

"They need someone to help lead the men's ministry."

"Tell me the guy I need to talk to."

Within three months I joined that church staff and took on the role of minister to men. My occupation became my vocation.

NEXT STEP

Men, as we wrap up this chapter I'd like for you not to be ashamed because you don't feel passion, but be inspired because you can. I'd like you to be certain that you matter, and that you absolutely influence people around you. Your North Star statement is a way of crystalizing that vision.

I want you to become utterly convinced that you are indeed on a noble journey. Your purpose in life has several aspects, each of them worthy to be lived to the fullest:

- You can have a greater sense of God's presence in your life moment by moment.
- You can make this world a better place for others by simple attitudes and actions you undertake every day.
- You have a life-long calling that is defined by your God-given Talent, by the People you care about, and by the Principle you want to live for.

May you take this to heart and then take the next step. Determine how you'd like to use your influence to touch your home, your workplace, your community, your church, and the world.

May the love of Christ compel you to action. You're on a noble journey and you matter.

QUESTIONS
FOR FURTHER THOUGHT OR DISCUSSION

1. Which of the Talents or Verbs listed in this chapter best describe how God made you?

2. Which of the People Groups best describe a concern or interest God has put on your heart?

3. Which of the Principles or Values describe something that compels you: You'd speak up for it; you'd be willing to get punished for it; you'd fight for it; you might even be willing to die for it?

4. Narrow your answers to the above to one or two words each. Use one of the templates in this chapter to write a first draft of a personal mission statement. Is it memorable and inspiring for you? What words are unnecessary? Scratch them out. What additional words simply must be included? Add them.

PART IV
GOD'S CHARGE
TO MEN

I n this last stage of our noble journey together, I want to make an in-depth exploration of a passage that remarkably encompasses the core theme of this book—you are on a critical path, one that determines whether your impact as a man is primarily self-centered or other-centered. Whether the legacy you pass on to others will be one that is defined by woundedness and destruction, or healing and blessing.

Toward the end of his first letter to the church at Corinth, Paul wrote: "Be on your guard; stand firm in the faith; be men of courage; be strong. Do everything in love" (1 Corinthians 16:13–14 NIV '84). Since he was writing to the whole church it's important to point out that his words were for women as well as men. But for us men, I want to lay out clearly what these words are saying specifically to us.

Verse 13 in English consists of just fifteen words but it is filled with significant meaning.

BE ON YOUR GUARD
What is it we are to guard? The answer can be found in one of the cornerstone verses of Scripture, Proverbs 4:23: "Above all else, guard your heart, for everything you do flows from it." Number one on our list, before we do anything else: guard our hearts. Why? Because our heart is the source of our life. It's where everything starts.

Our heart is the source of our purity: We need to guard it from sin. From the context of the passage in Proverbs it's clear the author is urging us to pursue purity in our words. "Put away perversity from your mouth, keep corrupt talk far from your lips."

It's easy for us to slide into coarse language, questionable jokes, or teasing that demeans others. Given the slippery morals promoted by TV shows and movies, it's easy to let our own thoughts and language start to slide. Given the snarky levels of derisive and demeaning anonymous communication online, it's almost natural to post a response that simply follows suit from the previous "bomb."

Allowing our minds to drift into lust is probably even more of a temptation for many of us. Statistics indicate that about 80% of men struggle with lust or pornography on some level. Of those, about 10% are consumed to the level of addictive behavior.

We have most likely already proven ourselves vulnerable to this. We must understand that the longing that compels men to pursue pornography, or real-life affairs, is actually a longing for connection, for significance, for intimacy, and for beauty. Every one of those longings is God-given, but we are pursuing them in broken ways.

We must recognize *where* we are vulnerable to the temptation to lust, and avoid it. We must recognize *when* we are vulnerable to the temptation of lust and guard it. We must pursue life-giving sources of satisfaction for our longings for connection and intimacy. And we must bring other men into our lives with whom we can share our journey and from whom we can receive support.

Our heart is the source of our joy: We need to guard it from anger. Anger in men is so common it's almost assumed that if you're a male you have to be grumpy, intimidating, distant, or sullen. As noted earlier, Neal Anderson writes, "Bitterness is the acid that eats its own container." Anne Lamott says, "Not forgiving is like drinking rat poison and then waiting for the rat to die" (*Traveling Mercies: Some Thoughts on Faith*).

Anger often results from blocked goals, unmet expectations, or a threat from someone or something around us. Anger is usually a sign that we have moved into self-preservation mode; it usually masks deeper emotions.

In most cases what lies beneath our anger is some form of fear: fear of failure, fear of rejection, and more than anything else for men, fear of not being respected. In response to these fears we resort to self-talk like:

- I MUST be respected by my wife and kids, so I'll demand it.
- I OUGHT to make more money, and nothing, or no one, better keep me from what I deserve.
- I SHOULD be the one chosen for the next promotion. Get out of the way.
- I SHOULD be a better Christian, so I'll impress others with my giving, my service, and my performance, but all the time resenting the expectations on me.

I must, I ought, I should. Living with these expectations makes for an angry man. As a friend of mine wisely says, "We need to stop 'shoulding' on ourselves." For the well-being of our hearts we need to let go of unrealistic expectations of ourselves and others.

We are urged, on the contrary, to have hearts filled with joy. There are more than 200 references in the Bible that urge us to be filled with joy and to live joyfully.

Our heart is the source of our inspiration: We need to guard it from depletion. All of us experience settings or know people who drain us:

- Work obligations, or choices on our own part, where unhealthy hours deplete us
- Broken relationships that drain us—ones we need to restore, or change before they drain us further
- Unrealistic demands we place on ourselves, putting us in a position of feeling unable to measure up
- Lies of the Enemy we listen to and accept, causing us to think we will never be good enough for God

Let's look at these a bit more. Guarding your heart means setting boundaries on our work hours, or saying "No" to certain obligations. This includes honestly evaluating why we are always saying "Yes" when it's killing us.

Jesus is a wonderful model of a man who knew when to say "Yes" and when to say "No." Scripture demonstrates that he had a sacred rhythm that governed his life. He moved from the restoration of solitude to the encouragement of community to the impact of outreach. But he knew when to focus on each.

Guarding our heart means setting boundaries on destructive relationships until we and the people involved can repair them. I have a friend whose mother-in-law was constantly criticizing and pointing out his weaknesses. He and wife put up with this treatment for years, but eventually my friend and his wife realized the mother-in-law's harsh comments were not just harming their relationship, they were destroying his heart.

In response he built an iceberg of resentment toward her. Finally, he and his wife agreed they needed to draw some boundaries. They sat down with her and the husband hesitantly but firmly said, "Mother, we love you, we want you to visit our home, and we want you in our kids' lives. But as long as you cut me down and criticize me you are not welcome here. The choice to be with us and the grandkids is yours, but we are establishing the conditions. When you're ready to stop demeaning me we'll invite you back."

That's speaking the truth in love! In order to resolve conflict and to maintain healthy relationships we need to speak both.

Guarding our heart means setting boundaries on our unrealistic demands on ourselves. Remember, our value as a man lies solely in the fact that God himself considers us his beloved sons. We don't need to keep placing expectations on ourselves to live up to others' standards. For those of us in Christ, we already meet God's!

Guarding our heart means setting boundaries on the lies of the Enemy that we listen to, and consent to. "You're not good enough. You'll never measure up. You're defective like no one else. No one cares about you anyway." The Enemy will do everything in his power to deplete us, discourage us, or dump us on the sidelines of our own lives. He wants us standing silently and passively while our families and friends long for our engagement.

We need to reject his lies that destroy our hearts and spirits. We need to draw a boundary against them by claiming powerful verses such as 1 John 4:4, "You, dear children, are from God and have overcome them, because the one who is in you is greater than the one who is in the world."

Guarding our hearts also means proactively pursuing those settings, activities, and relationships that are life-giving to us. Sometimes we disregard the crucial priority of finding time to restore our souls. Or we assume those pursuits are best kept for weekends or vacations alone. The Enemy doesn't wait for weekends and vacations in order to kill our joy or inspiration. He works around the clock. That's why it's a worthy priority for us to make time on a regular basis for those activities, hobbies, and settings that give us life. Here are a few:

- Art, which reflects the beauty of God
- Music, which can move us to tears or laughter
- Exercise, which brings our bodies alive
- Creation—mountains, water, desert, wildlife, trees, sun, which reveal the majesty and glory of the Creator
- Adventure, which transports us into the realms of courage and exhilaration
- Photography, which captures the light, composition, and color of life
- Reading and writing, which open the mind and heart to new ideas, perspectives, and stories

STAND FIRM IN THE FAITH

The second phrase in 1 Corinthians 16:13 is, "Stand firm in the faith." Oh, how we need to cling to those words. We must do all we can to understand and apply them.

Some of you, like me, remember growing up in the 60s. Some say, "If you can remember the 60s, you weren't really there." Well, I can say that I managed to avoid alcohol, drugs, and sex during my formative teen years, but there were near misses in some cases. I remember that era very well—with a smile and with tears.

Looking back, I view that decade as a time of almost unparalleled instability in our nation. It was a time of revolution and conflict only eclipsed by the Civil War. Everything I thought was solid ground began splitting apart as if hit by an earthquake:

- The United States only fights just wars, and always wins them. Not in Vietnam, where we lost more than 55,000 young men and women, and left in disgrace and embarrassment.
- American presidents are heroic paragons of integrity. Not during the Watergate years.
- Young people love their country and obey authorities unquestioningly. Not those who fled to Canada to live out their convictions or to avoid the draft.
- We are a nation where everyone is free and respects one another. Not those who are sent to the back of the bus or are refused entry to "white businesses."

President Kennedy was assassinated, then his brother Bobby, and then Martin Luther King, Jr. Great swatches of American cities were burnt to the ground during race riots. Everything I believed in was falling apart.

The economic, political, domestic, and international issues I read in the headlines today remind me of those unstable times. What can we count on anymore?

In the midst of this volatile reality we are challenged by Paul to stand firm. If we're honest we have to admit our reactions are often the same as those who have little or no faith. We may experience the same reactions that most everyone does when going through calamity:

- Gut emotional response: shock, panic, dread, fear, shame
- Creeping powerlessness: feeling paralyzed because what we face is too big, feeling alone and powerless in a vast sea
- Visceral rage: anger against the system, rage at those who failed us, anger at God for abandoning us
- Pointless floundering: trying one solution after another, jumping at anything

How do we stand firm in times like this? Psalm 20:7–8 gives us the proper perspective: "Some trust in chariots and some in horses, but we trust in the name of the LORD our God. They are brought to their knees and fall, but we rise up and stand firm."

Here's what this verse says to us today: "Some trust in chariots…" Chariots were the high technology of the day; an advanced means of transportation and a weapon of war. An equivalent reliance for us today would be an over-dependence on technology. Trusting that our cleverness, intellect, and modern systems will get us through any challenge.

On the contrary, our growing dependence on technology only makes us increasingly vulnerable. Military leaders warn us that the wars of the future will be cyber wars. The United States and our allies, with our abundance of high-tech weaponry, are the ones who are most vulnerable.

Technology betrays us on a regular basis. In 2016, two years after the fact, Yahoo disclosed that 500 million of its user accounts had been hacked in 2014. In March of 2017, they admitted that one billion accounts were compromised in a different attack in 2013 (March 15 *NY Times*). Technology has brought us enormous ability to communicate and learn; it has also brought exceptional complexity and vulnerability to our lives.

Psalm 20 goes on to say, "Some trust in horses." Horses were the most powerful animals of biblical times. Even today we measure power and strength by horsepower. A parallel meaning for us would be to put our trust in sheer effort and force of will. "I will put in whatever time and effort it takes, pay whatever price I have to, or that my family has to pay. I will figure this thing—financial security, career changes, medical needs—out and make it work. I will survive. In fact, I will thrive!"

Effort is commendable, God invented work, and we should never allow ourselves to be lazy or paralyzed with fear. But again, if we think sheer effort or cleverness on our part is going to be the primary source of our success we are relying on chariots and horses.

Exodus 14:10–14 recounts the story of Moses having taken the Israelites out of slavery in Egypt. Unfortunately, they then became lost in the desert, were chased by soldiers, and soon found themselves on the edge of the Red Sea. Essentially, they were between a hard army and a wet place.

They experienced the same emotions we do when threatened. Verse 11 illustrates visceral rage, or we might even call it dripping sarcasm:

"What! Were there not enough graves in Egypt that you had to bring us here to bury us?" Verse 12 illustrates creeping powerlessness: "Why did you bring us here? We'd rather be slaves in Egypt than die in the desert!"

Look at Moses' response in verses 13 and 14, "Do not be afraid. Stand firm and you will see the deliverance the LORD will bring you today...The LORD will fight for you; you need only to be still." As we learned long ago in Sunday school, God parted the sea and the Israelites were delivered from Pharaoh's army, upon whom the walls of water came crashing down.

When things look desperate, the Lord tells us to stand firm on what we believe. We must remember who God is and what his character is.

In *Let Your Life Speak*, Parker Palmer describes what he calls "Functional Atheism:"

It's...the belief that ultimate responsibility for everything rests with us. This is the unconscious, unexamined conviction that if anything decent is going to happen here, we are the ones who must make it happen—a conviction held by people who talk a good game about God.

When we take things into our own hands and ignore God's sovereign intent we are acting like functional atheists. We may talk a good game about God, but doubt his reliability or his interest in our circumstances. Our response to the trials and uncertainties of life reveals—in fact *proves*—what we believe about God. The best foundation for our trust and confidence is in *Jehovah-jireh*, the Lord who provides.

We will certainly experience trials and hardship. We will no doubt encounter loss, especially as we get older. Many of us will go through change in vocation or lifestyle. All of these are disruptive and upsetting. But that does not need to be the end of the story. We can live with the conviction, "I Trust You God." And he says through his Word, "Do not be afraid or discouraged. You will not have to fight this battle. I will deliver you."

BE MEN OF COURAGE

Our word "courage" comes from the French word *coeur*, or "heart." To be men of courage is to be men who live from the heart. Courage rises to the surface when, in the face of fear, we allow faith, conviction and heart, to guide us. This takes us back to the beginning where I talked about why we need to guard our hearts.

In chapter four we explored the best examples of a courageous man in the Old Testament, Joshua, who helped guide the children of Israel during their years wandering in the wilderness. In calling Joshua, God repeated the same phrase several times: "Be strong and courageous."

It's quite possible, perhaps likely, that Joshua was feeling the same way his mentor, Moses, felt when given this mantle of leadership. Moses made every excuse in the book as to why he couldn't or shouldn't accept it:

- Lord, who am I? (Exodus 3:11)
- Lord, who are you? (Exodus 3:13)
- Lord, what if they don't believe me? (Exodus 4:1)
- Lord, I don't speak well. (Exodus 4:10)
- Lord, can't you just get someone else to do it? (Exodus 4:13)

How do we feel when given a task, responsibility, or leadership role we feel somewhat unqualified for? What message do we need to hear and remember? "Be strong and very courageous. Wherever you go, I am going with you."

Joshua had a partner named Caleb who accompanied him to spy out the land of Canaan, along with ten other men. When they returned, the majority of them reported: "We went into the land to which you sent us, and it does flow with milk and honey! Look, here is its fruit. But the people who live there are powerful, and the cities are fortified and very large" (Numbers 13:27–28). They expressed somewhat understandable fear.

But verse 30 tells us that Caleb had a different view: "We should go up and take possession of the land, for we can certainly do it."

The other ten spies shot back: "We can't attack those people; they are stronger than we are…All the people we saw there are of great size."

And then these key words, "We seemed like grasshoppers in our own eyes, and we looked the same to them" (vv. 31–33).

God had promised Israel land and blessing, and the spies admitted, "Yes, it's a wonderful place." But they were intimidated by the threats they had seen. Not only did they exaggerate the size of the opponent, they diminished their own size, and as a result, God's: "We are like grasshoppers, and we look the same to them."

Their report causes so much anguish and fear in the assembly that Numbers 14:1–2 says they "raised their voices and wept aloud…If only we had died in Egypt! Or in this wilderness! Wouldn't it be better to go back to Egypt? We should choose a leader and go back!"

Perhaps we've expressed similar words in the face of fear, "How could God have led me to this mess? There are giants in front of me! I am just a grasshopper in the face of the challenges I'm confronting. I'd rather God had just left me where I was! At least I knew what my fate was!"

Early in my ministry career I was elevated to a level of responsibilities that stretched me on almost a daily basis. I was quite young for the role and I supervised older men and women who had at one time been instrumental mentors to me. I was very uneasy in this role.

"I seem like a grasshopper; and I look the same to everyone else." Though I didn't speak these words, they absolutely expressed how I felt on many occasions.

One of those men, a former teacher of mine and 25 years my senior, wrote me a note one day. I went to the safety of my office/man-cave and read it. "Craig, don't let anyone look down on you because you are young, but set an example for the believers in speech, in conduct, in love, in faith and in purity (1 Timothy 4:12). Glenn."

Not long after receiving that note I was asked to speak to a large group of ministry leaders and professors at The Billy Graham Center at Wheaton Graduate School. Man, did I feel like a grasshopper in frightening territory! I wondered, "What in the world do I have to offer these seasoned professionals?"

The only answer I could come up with was, "Don't apologize for your youth…set an example." I spoke on this very passage, Numbers

13 and 14, emphasizing God's ability to work beyond our limitations.

More than a few people came to me afterward and told me that story was a new source of insight and inspiration for them in overcoming fear. Who knew?

The book of Joshua gives a fuller account of how Joshua and Caleb responded. They stood up, tore their clothes, and said:

The land we passed through and explored is exceedingly good. If the LORD is pleased with us, he will lead us into that land, a land flowing with milk and honey, and will give it to us. Only do not rebel against the LORD. And do not be afraid of the people of the land, because we will devour them. Their protection is gone, but the LORD is with us. Do not be afraid of them. (Numbers 14:7–9)

These two men saw and felt the same things the other ten men who had explored the land did. They didn't somehow overlook the threatening tribes in the new land. They knew there would be a battle. But they focused on God's calling, his guidance, and the potential blessing rather than their weakness.

The Israelites did enter the Promised Land eventually but because of their unique trust and courage, Joshua and Caleb were the only adults alive the day the spies gave their report who ever saw it. The men who gave a bad report died of the plague; every other adult died in the wilderness, never to see the land of Canaan.

How do we become men of courage like Joshua and Caleb?

First, we trust: We do not deny fear; we admit it to the Lord. The Psalms are filled with David's heartfelt moaning; his pleading that God would release him from his fears. "How long, oh Lord, how long?" Some of us can say "Amen" to that. But we can also trust God and decide to believe him when he told us he would never forsake us and believe that he is sovereign).

Second, we obey: Having trusted what God says and who he is, we move forward. We engage despite our fears.

Trust and obey. It sounds like a song some of us sang in Sunday school a long time ago. What a simple message it communicates. Turns out it's true:

Blessed is the man who fears the LORD, who finds great delight in his commands...Surely he will never be shaken; a righteous man will be remembered forever. He will have no fear of bad news; his heart is steadfast, trusting in the LORD. His heart is secure, he will have no fear; in the end he will look in triumph on his foes. (Psalm 112:1, 6–8 NIV '84)

Who are the giants, and what are the circumstances that make us feel like grasshoppers? We need to identify the answers to these questions. And then we need to personalize the same message the Lord gave Joshua: "Be strong and courageous; I will be with you wherever you go. Just be strong and courageous."

When we listen to that message and truly take it to heart we can respond the same way Caleb and Joshua did:

> Only...do not rebel against the LORD. And do not be afraid of the people of the land, because we will devour them. Their protection is gone, but the LORD is with us. Do not be afraid of them. (Numbers 14:9)

BE STRONG

I live just north of Colorado Springs not far from the U.S. Air Force Academy. One of the sights that thrill most who live here is watching pilots training in gliders over the Academy property at the base of the front range of the Rocky Mountains.

With the right external lift, a glider seems capable of endless flight with no visible power of its own. That's the image I have in mind when I read this challenge: Be strong. Really, Lord? What about when I have no visible means of power? "Yes," he replies. "Exactly then; be strong."

Do you feel weak? Encountering adversaries that seem overwhelming? Aware of your own limitations? Seriously in need of a heavenly cheerleader? The angel of the Lord says to you, "Be strong and courageous. God is with you."

Like you, other men of God have felt in need of strength from a source beyond themselves. The apostle Paul himself was aware of his shortcomings. In 2 Corinthians 12 he boasts about God's sufficiency. He will not boast about himself except of his own weakness.

To keep him from becoming conceited, Paul says God gave him, "a thorn in the flesh." This wound or infirmity of some sort wasn't going away, either. Does Paul hide this weakness? No, he points it out; he brags about it. He is proud of the way God steps into his own weakness and brings strength:

> But he said to me, "My grace is sufficient for you, for my power is made perfect in weakness." Therefore, I will boast all the more gladly about my weaknesses...for when I am weak, then I am strong." (2 Corinthians 12:9–10)

The secret to a real man's strength is when he comes to the end of himself and then leans into God's strength. What does that mean to "come to the end of ourselves?" It means we:
- Confess the limits to our insights
- Admit to confusion
- Embrace, or even boast about, our weakness
- Quit fighting for our way

Paul is not giving us permission to bail when we encounter resistance, especially when there are others at home, work, or church who are relying on us. We show up, we are dependable for others; we act with integrity and courage. But we do not regard ourselves as the ultimate savior for others or ourselves. We acknowledge weakness. We trust God. And we act.

The above principles remind me of a time a colleague and I "came to the end of ourselves" while smuggling Bibles into Romania, one of the most repressive regimes in Eastern Europe back in the 1970s. Our vehicle designers had used all of their expertise to conceal 2,000 Bibles behind false wooden walls and linoleum floor tiles in our van.

We crossed the border with no undo attention from the guards and made contact with a pastor who happily agreed to receive and distribute the literature. Because he had no car of his own, we pulled up to his home at midnight to make the transfer as quickly as possible and then get out.

Everything was going according to plan—until headlights appeared in the street, and the car they belonged to slowly pulled up to our rear bumper. The moon cast just enough light for us to identify the blue and white colors of "Milicia"—Police!

The pastor scrambled back into his house. My colleague jumped into the front seat and pulled the curtains, closing off the view of the remaining black plastic bags jammed with about 1,000 Bibles. We were no longer in control. We were completely exposed and vulnerable. We prayed for God's protection and awaited what was to come.

The officer took our passports and asked what American tourists were doing in his town at night. ("I think we're lost, officer. Can you help?") He demanded we open the back doors and we knew without a doubt we were indeed "lost" and heading to jail.

When the doors were opened he stared with saucer-like eyes. "What is in the bags?" he demanded. I answered completely honestly: "Romanian Bibles we'd like to give to your countrymen. May we?"

The utter outrageousness of what we were doing, along with my request, must have short-circuited his brain because he then said something we never expected to hear from a policeman finding a van full of contraband. "What? No! You must immediately leave Romania!"

I couldn't believe it! He should have said, "You're under arrest!" He should have asked, "Who are you giving these to?" He didn't. He simply, inexplicably, ordered us to leave the country...with the Bibles still in our possession. And the next day we did.

Ordinarily we would have buried the Bibles in a forest for the next team to get on the next trip. But in this case, if the police officer called ahead to the border, we had to have the Bibles. We stuffed them into every cupboard, drawer, and closet to moderately conceal them in case the guards didn't look too closely, but they would be easy to find if the guards did. We pulled up to the border station and prayed for God's protection.

It became obvious the guards had not been told of our contraband when the first one opened the back door, and then a closet stacked floor to ceiling with Bibles. He slowly turned to me and asked in a bewildered tone, "You're taking these *out* of Romania?"

He called the station commandant, who likewise couldn't believe his eyes, or my story. My colleague and I once again awaited the arrest and imprisonment. But then the commandant asked with a sly grin, "What border did you cross yesterday?" He probably planned to report the negligent officer controlling whatever station we had smuggled this literature through.

"This one," I said. He shook his head and grabbed my passport. "Not possible!" he yelled. "You did not cross through my station!" He found the visa stamp, and there it was: his border station. He had failed in his most important job. He turned white, tossed our passports back, and said through clenched teeth, "Get out of Romania!"

My colleague and I happily did as requested, shaking our heads in wonder at God's protection when we were at our weakest.

That was one of the clearest examples we ever had where our intellect, our planning, and our efforts—our strength, in other words—came to their obvious limit. We could only let go, rest in God's sovereignty, and see what he might do. What he did was completely beyond our ability to pull off.

DO EVERYTHING IN LOVE

Up to this point we've unpacked the four phrases in 1 Corinthians 16:13. They are reassuring encouragement and powerful reminders of our calling as men: to be on our guard, to stand firm, to be courageous and strong. These phrases make sense to us. They sound masculine. We may not do all of them well, but we aspire to be like these descriptions.

And then comes verse 14: "Do everything in love." I beg your pardon? Love? What does that have to do with strength, courage, standing firm? Having grabbed our attention, Paul now turns the message upside down and inside out. Verse 13 has focused on our inner qualities. But love? As we saw in much more detail in chapter 5, the direction of love in a noble man is always outward; it's always other-centered.

If we're honest, we have to admit our attitude is consistently inward—our well-being, our security, our success. We are often tempted to be self-centered; to believe life is primarily about us. Paul is telling us to do the opposite.

This transition, moving from a self-centered perspective of life to an other-centered focus is the primary distinguishing factor that sets apart noble men from selfish men. *It is the distinguishing quality that separates men from boys.*

In 2008 Michael Kimmel wrote a fascinating book entitled *Guyland*, about North American male culture. In it he describes Guyland as a sub-set of males (I refrain from calling them men; they are not-yet-men) in the 16–26 age group who have never grown up. In conducting more than 1,000 interviews with high school, college, and post-college young people, he defines this sub-culture as self-absorbed, woman-demeaning, party-centric boys, largely consumed by the pursuit of drinking, sex and video games.

This class of young males has been trained to be irresponsible, narcissistic, and entitled. This description comes as no surprise to their parents and to most of the women in this age group. It's the reason so many young women ask, "Where are all the good men?"

The worldview of this sub-culture—it's all about me—is apparent in how they spend their time and money and how they conduct their relationships. Our culture gives them permission to live this way and conveys the message that this is what real men are like.

Scripture tells us quite the opposite. I can't think of a passage that looks more upside down to our culture than Philippians 2:3–8. If we have any interest in being like Jesus, then it's clear what that looks like:

- Don't do anything out of selfish ambition
- Consider others better than yourselves
- Don't look only to what benefits you, but also to what benefits others

Our attitude should be the same as that of Jesus:

- Although he was God, he didn't demand honor or respect
- On the contrary, he made himself nothing

- He took on human appearance and confined himself to the limits of flesh and blood
- He went further, he became a servant of all
- He went further still, he was obedient to the point of death
- He even went further, he humbled himself to death on the cross; the most humiliating and painful form of execution known at the time

The truth of this passage sheds light on how we can apply verses 13 and 14 of 1 Corinthians 16. The *self-absorbed shadow male* is on guard. He looks out for himself. He rarely stands firm. He wavers, waiting to see which side is going to win before taking his stand. His courage and strength are false bravado and posing. In the face of fear he intimidates, powers up, or shrinks back and disappears.

On the other hand, the *noble man* is on guard on behalf of others. He stands firmly on what he believes, and for whom he loves. He courageously acts in the face of fear in order to defend others, and he uses his strength in a gentle humble way for the protection of others.

A noble man is willing to trust God with the results of his life. He knows his life ultimately is not about him. It's about bringing glory to God. It's about being transformed into the image of Christ. It's about being present and engaged for the benefit of others.

Be on your guard.

Stand firm in the faith.

Be men of courage; be strong.

Do everything, everything, everything in love.

This is God's charge to men. It's not an impossible to-do list, though we are aware of our shortcomings. God wrote these qualities on every man's heart; he built these characteristics into *you*. Bring them up from your heart, soul, mind, and strength. This is a man's noble journey. And where you fall short, God is there. Trust him to do above and beyond what you can do in your own ability.

In conclusion, let me offer this prayer of blessing: *A Prayer by Saint Benedict for Seekers of Faith.* As we humbly trust God to increasingly reveal these characteristics in our lives, may we be empowered by the grace and strength he has placed in us:

Almighty God, give us wisdom to perceive you,
intelligence to understand you,
diligence to seek you,
patience to wait for you,
vision to behold you,
a heart to meditate upon you,
a love to proclaim you;
through Jesus Christ our Lord,
who lives with you and the Holy Spirit,
one God now and forever.

Lord, be with us to guide us,
within us to strengthen us,
without us to protect us,
above us to raise us,
beneath us to uphold us,
before us to lead us,
behind us to guard us,
ever about us,
this day and evermore;
this day and evermore.

Amen.

May we invite the guidance of the Father's hand on our quest to pass on a lasting legacy to others—this day and evermore.

QUESTIONS
FOR FURTHER THOUGHT OR DISCUSSION

Be on your guard. Be vigilant for others.

Stand firm in the faith. Be consistently true to your convictions for the benefit of others.

Be men of courage. Stand up, speak up, act for those who are vulnerable.

Be strong. Use your gifts and acknowledge your limitations with those who rely on you.

Which of these qualities comes naturally to you? Which would you love to grow in?

About the Author

Craig Glass has served as Vice President of Ministries at International Teams, pastor to men at Willow Creek Community Church, and National Director of Field Ministries at International Students Incorporated. He is the founder and President of Peregrine Ministries with the mission to guide and inspire men on their life journey. He is the author of *Passage to Manhood Field Guide.* Craig and Beryl were married in 1976, have three children, five granddaughters, one grandson, and live in Monument, CO. In his free time Craig enjoys biking, golf, fly-fishing, and competitive swimming.

Contact Craig: craig@peregrineministries.org
Visit our website: www.peregrineministries.org
Follow us: www.facebook.com/menmatter.craigglass
Subscribe to the Men Matter Blog: www.menmattertoday.com

Also by Craig Glass

Dads of teenaged sons, grandfathers and youth leaders, the **Passage to Manhood Field Guide** presents a clear and compelling description of what it looks like to be a man based on the words of Jesus in Mark 12:30-31: "Love the Lord your God with all your *heart*, with all your *soul*, with all your *mind* and with all your *strength*... Love your neighbor as yourself." Learn how these four components define true manhood: Compassion, Confidence, Conviction, and Courage and how they are dynamically expressed through the roles of Lover, King, Mentor, and Warrior. This can be a discipling experience you will never regret, and your teen will never forget. The book is available at **www.peregrineministries.org** or **www.amazon.com**.

Recommended Resources

The Masculine Journey

Bly, Robert. *Iron John*. Addison-Wesley, 1990.

Crabb, Larry. *The Silence of Adam*. Zondervan, 1995.

Dalbey, Gordon. *Healing the Masculine Soul*. Word, 1988.

Eldredge, John. *Wild at Heart*. Thomas Nelson, 2001.

Glass, Craig M. *Passage to Manhood Field Guide*. Peregrine Ministries, 2016.

Kimmel, Michael. *Guyland*. HarperCollins, 2008.

MacDonald, Gordon. *When Men Think Private Thoughts*. Thomas Nelson, 1996.

Miller, Donald. *To Own a Dragon*. NavPress, 2006.

Rohr, Richard. *From Wild Man to Wise Man*. St. Anthony Messenger Press, 1990, 2005.

Smith, Stephen W. *The Transformation of a Man's Heart*. IVP Books, 2006.

Weber, Stu. *Tender Warrior*. Multnomah, 1993.

Significance, Identity, and Relationship with God

Benner, David. *The Gift of Being Yourself*. InterVarsity, 2004.

Crabb, Larry. *Inside Out*. Navpress, 1988.

Curtis, Brent, and John Eldredge. *The Sacred Romance*. Thomas Nelson, 1997.

Eldredge, John. *The Journey of Desire*. Thomas Nelson, 2000.

Lynch, John, and Bruce McNicol. *The Cure*. Crosssection, 2011.

Manning, Brennan. *The Ragamuffin Gospel*. Multonomah, 1990.

Nouwen, Henri. *The Way of the Heart*. HarperCollins, 1981.

Nouwen, Henri. *The Return of the Prodigal Son*. Doubleday, 1992.

Smedes, Lewis. *Shame and Grace*. Zondervan, 1993.

Taylor, Daniel. *In Search of Sacred Places*. Bog Walk Press, 2005.

Thrall, Bill, Brice McNicol, and John Lynch. *TrueFaced*. NavPress, 2003.

Purity and Sexual Temptation

Arterburn, Stephen, and Dred Stoeker. *Every Man's Battle.* Waterbrook, 2000.

Cusick, Michael. *Surfing for God.* Thomas Nelson, 2012.

Marriage and Parenting

Anderson, Michael, and Timothy Johanson. *Gist.* GISTWorks, 2013.

Crabb, Larry. *Men & Women: Enjoying the Difference.* Zondervan, 1991.

Eggerichs, Emerson. *Love & Respect.* Integrity Publishers, 2004.

Smalley, Gary, and Ted Cunningham. *From Anger to Intimacy.* Regal, 2009.

Thomas, Gary. *Sacred Marriage.* Zondervan, 2000.

Work and Calling

Barkalow, Gary. *It's Your Call.* David C. Cook, 2010.

Bolles, Richard. *How to Find Your Mission in Life.* Ten Speed Press, 1991.

Palmer, Parker. *A Hidden Wholeness.* Jossey-Bass, 2004.

Palmer, Parker. *Let Your Life Speak.* Jossey-Bass, 2000.

Smith, Stephen W. *Inside Job.* IVP Books, 2015.

Stanley, Andy. *Choosing to Cheat.* Multnomah, 2002.

Made in USA - Kendallville, IN
84540_9781976567957
12.14.2022 1431